Purchasing
Power

Purchasing
<u>Power</u>

YOUR SUPPLIERS, YOUR PROFITS

RICHARD RUSSILL

PRENTICE HALL

LONDON NEW YORK TORONTO SYDNEY TOKYO SINGAPORE
MADRID MEXICO CITY MUNICH PARIS

First published 1997 by
Prentice Hall Europe
Campus 400, Maylands Avenue
Hemel Hempstead
Hertfordshire HP2 7EZ
A division of
Simon & Schuster International Group

Typeset in 9½/12pt Melior by
Hands Fotoset, Ratby, Leicester

Printed and bound in Great Britain by
Redwood Books, Trowbridge, Wiltshire

Library of Congress Cataloging-in-Publication Data

Available from the publisher

British Library Cataloguing in Publication Data

A catalogue record for this book is available from
the British Library

ISBN 0-13-442625-8

1 2 3 4 5   01 00 99 98 97

Contents

Preface   *page* xi

Acknowledgements   xii

Introduction: Are these questions on your agenda?   1

Part I   3

1   Procurement . . . and the revival of better business   5
'Order-placement' taken to task   5
This book . . . and how to make good companies a great deal better   6
A profit paradox, competitiveness and corporate survival   7
   The beginnings of business   8
Turning new thinking into new reality   9
   How changing the procurement process can help: a painful but
     profound renaissance   9
   How small businesses get big, and into trouble   10
   How big businesses get small, and into trouble   12
The best of both worlds   14
   The 'Centrepreneur'   14
   Procurement renaissance   15
References   15

2   Core beliefs in a changing business world   16
Mindsets which can emancipate, or mar, corporate performance
Procurement's impact: specialism or profound influence   16
Trends in supply-side exposure   17

Procurement: its critical importance   19

Five core beliefs   20

The 'core beliefs' examined in detail   21

   First to have access   21

   Two aspects of internal teamwork   22

   Three-pronged action: image, approach and coordination   26

   Four pillars: tools, techniques, systems and controls 27

   A fifth dimension: the value of process   28

 A new 'investment opportunity'   29

   Positive costs   29

Summary   30

Reference   31

3   Essential to the success of the business   32
How to build towards the vision of better procurement practice

Procurement's role: 'if you believe . . . no proof is necessary'   32

Stairway to the process vision   33

   'Standards and control'   33

   'Prices are not fixed'   34

   'Profit contribution'   35

   'Contribution to other task results'   36

   Link procurement's role to the corporate strategy'   38

   'A primary business process'   39

Strategic procurement   39

4   Reviving commercial awareness   41
Why 'we are all buyers'

'Entrepreneurial, adj.: mindful of business'   41

Specifying needs versus prescribing solutions   41

Problems of 'a linear sequence' versus 'a shared process'   43

   Solution 1: stepwise through the procurement process   43

   Solution 2: an integrated mindset   44

5   How to eliminate waste and supply-chain costs   46

Total cost of ownership versus the total cost of bad behaviour   46

Three cost-reduction strategies: 47

   Control, focus and coordination of expenditures   47

Understanding and outmanoeuvring the supply market   48

Collaborating with selected suppliers on cost-reduction projects 49

Getting it together: the 'best' cost curve   50

The opportunity   51

Appendix: How wasteful costs get into supply chains   52

Reference   58

6 Towards better procurement practice   59

Today's cost-cut problems: being compounded by solutions?   59

Mission of the procurement process   60

It's not just what you say . . .   61

. . . But also the way you say it!   62

Current best practice defined   62

Mission   62

Policies and principles   62

Vision for the future   64

Reference   66

7 Organising for a high-performing procurement process   67

Organising time and priorities   67

What can go wrong with policies'?   67

Why downstream problems?   69

Defining and locating procurement tasks   70

Centralising procurement's muscle power   71

Keeping the buying local   72

'CLAN': the network platform for process leadership   73

Prerequisites for success   75

Route map for revolution   76

Beyond task to process leadership – and beyond that to leading the
way for change   77

References   77

8 Organising for process leadership   78

The task tradition   78

Towards 'preeminent organisational effectiveness'   79

Procurement: the instrument of change   80

Old companies, new tunes: how procurement writes the score   81

Process orchestration for 'preeminent effectiveness'   82

Evolution of cross-functional teams   84

New frontiers for the 'boundaryless' company . . . and how to avoid
old traps   85

References   87

9   Towards best, then better, practice: the challenge of change   88

Why initiatives are 'coming together'   88

Why change can be tragic   89

The real challenge: procurement renaissance   89

So what is needed?   91

How to rise above the barriers to change   91

Assembling the critical mass for change   92

Checklist for procurement renaissance   94

Good-buy to best practice   94

Part II   97

10   Good strategies are 'nice' strategies!   99

Template for strategic plan   100

Contents: the position paper   100

Strategic plan for the acquisition of 'X'   100

Why 'nice' strategies?   102

The tools and process to use   102

Appendix: Strategic procurement planning: 'Fastrack' strategy
development   104

11   The strategic planning tool kit   106

Supply positioning: opening windows on the supply market   106

Supplier preference overview: the view from the supply side   108

Adding one on one: the 'promised land', or Armageddon?!   109

Vulnerability analysis   109

So we've analysed the way it is: what next?   110

Instruments are for playing tunes . . . not making notes   117

References   117

12 Managing the supply interface – ten key questions   118

  1. Suppliers – where are they?   118

  2. How do we appear to them . . . and are they interested?   119

     But are they interested?   120

  3. Will they be any good?   120

  4. Who will be the main contact between our companies?   121

  5. How important are they, and their suppliers, to us?   122

  6. How should we approach them?   123

  7. How might we be tied together?   123

  8. With whom do we contract . . . and is it the best deal?   124

     First, how best is best?   124

     How do we choose which deal to accept?   126

     Awarding the contract   126

  9. How do we keep them under control?   127

 10. Was it OK?   128

 Appendix 'Clean-up on costs': a total-cost evaluation case study   129

13 Getting around price   133

 The total cost picture   133

 Getting round behind price   135

  Pricing policy and its objective   135

  Company pprofitability and financial status   135

  Price breakdown   136

  How desperately does the seller need your order?   137

  What do they think they can get?   137

  How effectively have they 'conditioned' you to agree with
   what they want?   138

  'Getting round behind price': Summary   139

 How best to improve a price proposal   140

 Managing price 'in future'   143

**14 Keeping costs out of supply chains . . . by ironing out
    market distortions**   146

 Why monopolies? . . . and what to do?   146

 Why cartels? . . . and what to do?   147

 But the true enemy is wasteful costs   149

15 How suppliers can add value   150

Sizing up supplier relationships   151

Eliminating wasteful costs . . . by joint problem-solving with
    motivated suppliers   152

    How to motivate suppliers   153

    Areas for the joint attack on wasteful costs   155

    Deciding who to work with   156

Key account management   157

    Satisfiers   158

    'KSAM': key supplier account management   158

References   159

16 Negotiation does not have to mean meeting halfway   160

Not win–win but won-round   160

    Methods of persuasion   161

Top targeting . . . and the 'F-squared' factor   162

Phases of negotiation . . . what's going on?   164

Four characteristics of successful negotiators   165

References   166

17 How to measure procurement impact   167

Who's interested?   168

What are we trying to prove?   171

The measurement hierarchy   173

The bottom line . . . and the last word   176

Appendix: Measurement 'à la carte'   177

Index   181

Preface

Purchasing, or procurement is most often talked about in terms of cost: doing it better means less cost and more profit. But this book goes further than that. It is not about making money but about helping business organisations to achieve their goals, not just for now but in a sustainable way. And if your business is a public sector activity where the goal is not to make profit but to provide service within budgets, then the object is to obtain excellent value from supply markets at the same time as beating cost targets. However, supply market value is measured not just in terms of lowest total cost but also reflects the value of innovation and preferential treatment which comes from a supplier who is truly aligned to a specific customer's goals. Such relationships never happen by chance but are born with care and nurtured thereafter by both parties. Then there is the darker side of the picture: helpless customers exposed to the pricing games and manipulations of distorted and hence uncompetitive supply markets. But is the buyer aware? If not, what is in fact a jungle is taken as a fool's paradise.

Revival and renaissance   Mostly though, this book is about re-creating in mature companies the high-performing behaviours that they exhibited when they were young, and to show still-young companies how to avoid the pitfalls of growth. In pursuing this aim, the 'procurement process' is advocated as one of the central value creators in business which has the rare ability to offer two prizes for one throw: profit and value contribution now *plus* business revival for the future. Truly, an opportunity to make already good companies a 'great deal' better.

> This book shows how to buy well, and how the process of change itself breathes new life into the enterprise: Procurement Renaissance.
> The real goal is not merely to copy best practice, but to create that core competence which maximises the chances of company survival long term . . . 'the ability to do new things better and faster than the competition'.

Acknowledgements

One of the great privileges of being a practitioner in a high-class multinational corporation, and then to work internationally with a wide variety of similarly classy companies from the consultancy side of the table as I have been fortunate to do . . . is the people you get to meet. The best part is when colleagues and clients also become friends. This in turn creates conditions in which new ideas get developed and already held and cherished ones get tested . . . sometimes, thankfully, to destruction. It's the questions, challenges and experiences provided by colleagues and clients alike which I appreciate as having stimulated much of the material in this book, and for this I am grateful. I feel passionately that there is a story to tell, and if you feel this book tells it successfully then you deserve your part of the credit.

I am especially indebted to a number of my consultancy colleagues whose ideas and anecdotes have contributed to this book, and whose conversation and *camaraderie* has stimulated new thinking and precipitated out new concepts which would otherwise have remained in suspension. I have named them throughout the book where the subject makes it appropriate. My heartfelt thanks to you all. But I would like to single out B. H. Court for special mention. Brian has been a valued friend and colleague throughout the industrial and consultancy phases of my professional life and has never failed to recognise instinctively the value of an embryo concept or to probe a shaky idea until it settled on to a more robust foundation. And he never stops creating and sharing new ideas of his own. It is a privilege to find someone who combines all this with high principles and a real concern for people and it is right that this acknowledgement should rejoice in our achievements and friendship.

I also learned much from the then Hong Kong-based business magazine *Electronic Components* (part of the Asian Sources Media Group) who were kind enough over a period of four recent years to get me to write a series of short articles under the heading 'The Purchasing Professional'. There's nothing like a deadline shouting for the next batch of 800 words to force the pace both in terms of creativity and page coverage. Their own subject ideas, snappy prose style, and blue-pencilled editorial discipline have indelibly made their mark on what follows. Thank you. It then seemed a natural progression for Prentice Hall to be so receptive to the idea to publish this book and I am most grateful for their unqualified support and expertise in bringing it to fruition.

Finally, my grateful thanks to Gary Cheesman, Richard May, Tom Medawar, Alison Sanderson and Adrian White who devoted valuable time to review the book and made such excellent suggestions as to how to improve it.

R. C. Russill
Hampshire, England, 1997

Introduction

Are these questions on your agenda?

1. Here is the core of one real company's P&L statement as published in their annual report. This is the way such figures are traditionally presented.

	$ million as %
Sales revenue	100.0
Operating expenses	(86.8)
Operating profit	13.2
Tax/interest, etc.	(5.9)
Trading profit	7.3

In your opinion, what are the reasons for doing it this way . . . and what impression is created by so doing?

See chapter 2 for a different and more revealing approach.

2. For many companies, the most productive way of improving profitability is to:

(a) reduce overheads and operating costs by 10 per cent
(b) reduce expenditures in the supply market by 5 per cent
(c) reduce labour costs by 15 per cent
(d) increase sales by 25 per cent

Please choose one only, **and then see chapter 3 for some new perspectives.**

3. How are we leveraging our company's size in our relationships with key suppliers, and what benefits do we derive from so doing?

Most companies go for 'Tactical Leverage' to get a lower price . . . but that's often all they do get. The smart companies use *brain* power as well as muscle power. **See chapter 9 to find out how Strategic Procurement** differs from Tactical Leverage, and **chapter 7 for the CLAN network approach** to organising global network management of the supply market.

4. 'If one of our suppliers develops a cost or quality innovation, or a brilliant new creative concept, would we be the first customer they call?'

These were the words used by the Chief Executive of a North American multi-national FMCG company when opening a global procurement conference. Can you hear your CEO saying the same thing?

If you can, that's great news and maybe they're now ready for

Procurement Renaissance **(chapter 10 for the way to get to best practice)**
If not, turn to chapter 1 fast . . . and then 2 . . . and then 3!

5. 'How do our suppliers assess our performance? Would we be considered their best customer?'

The same CEO again, demonstrating a best practice belief and attitude in wanting to excite and positively challenge key suppliers to achieve new realms of performance to mutual advantage. See that company's vision statement **(Vision 2 in chapter 6).**

But . . . can the same be said for your company?

6. Do you know who are your most important suppliers, and what criteria do you use to say so?

The knee-jerk answer is to say 'they are the ones with whom we spend most money'. But reality can be worryingly different. (Look at chapter 11 for fresh viewpoints.)

7. '*Negotiation*' is:

(a) the act of resolving conflict between two parties
(b) the use of logic to convince the other party
(c) fighting to get your own way
(d) a win/lose process
(e) a process for getting the other party to change its mind
(f) a compromise reached by discussion

Which definition most nearly fits your own view? Please choose one only.

Most people in the world choose (f) but can you do better? (Find out in chapter 16.)

8. You wish to acquire a new personal computer with full multi-media facilities. The make and type have already been decided. Each of three suppliers has offered prices as follows:

Dealer	A	B	C
Price	$7,100	$7,300	$7,295
Target			

Please write down your price target (expressed as a number or a percentage discount) for each dealer, in the spaces provided. Each supplier is offering precisely the same 'total' package.

Does your answer meet the 'Top-Targeting' test? **(See chapter 16 to find out.)**

Now read on . . . and I really hope you enjoy this book!

Part I

Chapter one

Procurement . . . and the revival of better business

■ 'Order-placement' taken to task

In its narrowest sense, procurement, better defined at this level as 'order-placement', is seen as a mechanistic transaction. A company's need for services or materials (often specified separately by someone else in the business) is thus satisfied by a supplier whose commitment to supply is engaged via a legally binding contract. In this scenario the buyer's involvement starts when the need is announced by a 'requisition', and stops once the order is placed. Ongoing contact with the supplier, both pre- and

---

Table 1.1

Without an 'organised' approach to procurement there can, typically, be

Total supply-side expenditure >5–10 per cent more than it need be
(inflicting direct damage to profit and cash)

plus

Three or more of the following:

Beaten by competitors to the market with new ideas, products or services
Customers kept waiting or turned down
Output prices forced up with loss of competitiveness
Insufficient 'internal challenge' in supply-side specifications and decision-making
Decision-makers prey to the tactics of salespeople
Unproductive use of human resources
Fragmentation and loss of leverage
Political embarrassment
Vulnerability to fraud
Legally unsound contracts heavily biased in suppliers' favour
Exploited and manipulated by monopolies and cartels
Poor supplier performance or, worse, allocation or loss of supply
Supplier innovations passed to competitors

After you've worked so hard to win the customers do you really want to throw away hard-earned sales revenue like this?

---

post-contract is someone else's business. This is an acute form of task partitioning within the company. The problem is that all the 'someone elses', equally focussed on the task, are unaware that they are engaged in commercially sensitive *relationships* in which supplier performance and the cost-effectiveness of the deal are hugely influenced by the behaviour of the customer company, acting as a corporate team and as individuals. There is a widespread belief that once you've specified what you want, then price and cost follow as a matter of course. The truth is otherwise. It is the *way* the supply market is understood and played which makes at least an equal impact. This is why the best private and public sector businesses, in pursuit of getting even better, are now placing so much emphasis on creating a high-performing company-spanning 'procurement process'. Ignoring these facts can inflict much damage on business performance. Table 1.1 illustrates what happens if 'procurement' is not taken seriously.

■ This book . . . and how to make good companies a great deal better

Procurement is most often talked about in terms of cost: doing it better means less cost and more profit. But this book goes further than that. It is not about making money but about helping business organisations to achieve their goals – not just for now but in a sustainable way. And if your business is a public sector activity where the goal is not to make profit but to provide service within budgets, then the object is to obtain excellent value from supply markets at the same time as beating cost targets. However, supply market value is measured not just in terms of lowest total cost but also reflects the value of innovation and preferential treatment which come from a supplier who is truly aligned to a specific customer's goals. Such relationships never happen by chance but are born with care and nurtured thereafter by both parties. Then there is the darker side of the picture: helpless customers exposed to the pricing games and manipulations of distorted and hence uncompetitive supply markets. But is the buyer aware? If not, what is in fact a jungle is taken as a fool's paradise.

Revival and renaissance

Mostly though, this book is about recreating in mature companies the high-performing behaviours that they exhibited when they were young. It will also show still-young companies how to avoid the pitfalls of growth. In pursuing this aim, the procurement process is advocated as one of the central value-creators in business which has the rare ability to offer two prizes for one throw: profit and value contribution now plus business revival for the future. Truly an opportunity to make already good companies a 'great deal' better.

The book comes in two parts. Part I comprises chapters 1–9 and sets out the business case by placing the procurement process in the context of the overall company. It shows how issues such as authority, empowerment, control, organisation and cross-functional collaboration are interpreted in today's acutely cost-aware business environment of seemingly constant re-structuring, process management, devolved activity, and networking. Perhaps even more important for starters is that it shows how to win round hearts and minds to seeing procurement as a key business process and not merely the lost world of back-office clerks. In this way Part I builds the platform upon which to conduct a high-class procurement performance. But what about the instruments and orchestration? These and more are the subjects of Part II where issues such as strategic planning, decision-making tools, cost and price management and many 'how-to's' are set out. Tips on dealing with monopolies, cartels and negotiation are included.

However, a word of warning. Part II practicalities will only deliver best results if applied in a business environment as described in Part I. Only by creating this platform, recognisable amongst other things by the fact that 'commerciality' will be clearly evident in everyone's decisions and behaviour, will the company fully benefit from the renaissance: entrepreneurial behaviour harmonised with the needs of corporate goals and accountability. Or, as a jazz music critic put it: 'everyone doing their own thing according to plan!'

■ A profit paradox, competitiveness and corporate survival

Old business hands and young start-ups

Why distinguish between 'old' company and 'young' company behaviours? Because there appears to be a widely observable paradox in business behaviour. Many organisations spend an inordinate amount of time and effort on earning revenues or winning budgets, and then effectively squander that effort through wasteful expenditure of hard-won money. 'Waste' does not just mean spending on things which are not really wanted. More often it means expending far too much on things which ARE needed. Most often the culprit is 'wrong behaviour' on the part of the individuals and the corporate team overall, although wrong specifications also play their part in damaging the bottom line. It's as if the money *in*flows from revenue generation are differently regarded from money *out*flows at the supply market end of the business. In many minds the trading-margin calculations try to equate 'chalk with cheese' despite the fact that capturing an additional money unit at either end of the business will equally enhance gross margin. Conversely, the 'young company' can be seen to be keeping a keen eye on both ends of the margin. And more: the supply end of the business is seen as offering value-creation and more scope for cost control than can be achieved by passing on rising costs to capricious customers. As one 'young' company (albeit in business for more than 70 years and with more than 3,300 valued people in the global corporate team) puts it: 'we make our business by selling to our customers, but we make our profit from procurement'. Yes, they realise this is an over-simplification, but it makes the point as regards their balanced view of priorities. But their Group Vice-President, Procurement, goes further when discussing how to measure procurement performance:

> We are not too concerned at having to prove or justify by calculation the need to take procurement seriously . . . it is accepted as being essential to our success and our concern is how to do it as well as possible.   (Group Vice-President, multinational company)

Meanwhile back in the 'old' companies the squeeze on margins heralds the onset of major cost-reduction initiatives and a lasting preoccupation with internal cost control. Somehow it is assumed that, apart from leveraging price reductions wherever possible, external costs in the supply market cannot be so influenced (note that if this is the case then a successful salesperson has been at work). The danger is that over-concentration on cost reduction, especially when allied to 'outsourcing', can lead to a hollowing out of the heart of the business, doing little if anything to enlarge business capability or competitiveness.

> OK, you've proved you can cut costs . . . now show you can grow the business.
>
> (Recent *Fortune* magazine header)

Only very few have recognised, rediscovered even, that the smart view of the supply market is not just to see it as the external provider of resources needed for today's business but also as the source of tomorrow's business competitive edge . . . competitive edge in terms of being better than the rest in achieving corporate goals and surviving long term. But why talk in terms of 're-discovery'? Read on.

The beginnings of business

A company President was introducing an in-company conference aimed at enhancing cross-functional collaboration throughout the procurement process. The company was, and is, investing vast sums in capital projects and was thus concerned to manage cash flow so that capital funds were available without seeking loans. 'The best way to improve cash flow is not to spend money at all,' he said, 'but since we have to, then we need a good buying team in place to manage it for us. That's why this conference is important.' **Good news . . . and bad news**.

The good news was that a senior executive was advocating procurement's case. The bad news was that the message was the wrong one. His view betrayed a perception that spending money in the supply market is an inevitable, perhaps undesirable, consequence of being in business. In truth it is the other way round – ask any entrepreneur or small business owner.

Companies start up because an opportunity is seen at the output end of the enterprise (e.g. a customer need) that can be satisfied by obtaining something at the input end, from the supply market. The entrepreneur makes a margin by passing it on at a mark-up – often, but not necessarily, adding some value in the process.

A fact of business life
Spending money in a supply market in the right way is a **prerequisite** for being in business, not an **undesirable consequence**.

Alternatively a supply opportunity presents itself and the entrepreneur creates a market for it. Either way, having access to excellent suppliers as well as customers is what enables small companies to start up and grow.

■ Turning new thinking into new reality

Small businesses are back in. The company which provides the setting for the above story is multi-national with total employees worldwide of more than forty thousand. However it is not organised as a tall hierarchical pyramid but as a network of small companies. Some world-spanning businesses now refer to themselves as 'federations'. Large companies made up of small ones become possible because for the first time for a long time the CEO can see both ends of a vast business at the same time, courtesy of information technology. Margins, and the opportunities for procurement to increase them, are more visible. By devolving into strategic business units, big companies are transforming themselves into networks of small ones.

This trend and a number of other issues are coming together in a clear way for the first time. Empowerment is 'in' at the personal level. The need for collaboration and synergy across functions and across businesses is answered by the call for Business Process Reengineering (BPR), itself derived from the well-understood but not often practised philosophy that 'best' task results can only be achieved by effective management of process. And 'best' is what the already good companies are envisioning they will become in future. Only by reaching out for that goal will they retain competitive advantage. Best-Practice Benchmarking is relied on to check how well they make progress. One common theme running through these popular 'initiatives' is that they all aim to revitalise entrepreneurial decision-making within the company. Would that this were so! Unfortunately the declared goal is often less altruistic and more short term: to cut costs. This leads to the inevitable conclusion that the fewer people left on the payroll have to have more authority for action just to keep the wheels turning. However, whether by design or not, all such initiatives in a sense seek to recreate the climate of a small company within the framework of a large one.

But the problem is that many new concepts and initiatives are difficult to realise in practice and the vast sums often spent on implementing them are then doubted in the light of questionable improvements in real business results. One reason is that the grand plan is often applied on only a small scale. For example the invoice-payment process is often targeted for reengineering (and often needs it). The size of the task and it's describable nature makes it a natural candidate for BPR methodology. But no company is going to become world-best just by fixing an invoice-payment problem. A larger change is needed. How can this be achieved?

How changing the procurement process can help: a painful but profound renaissance

The procurement process is a microcosm of the business overall in that it embraces the activities of corporate planners, budget providers, budget holders managing their allotted lines of business, buyers, users at the receiving ends of supply lines, sales-people who allow for supply costs in their own price calculations, finance and so on. As one CEO puts it,

> Procurement spans all aspects of our business. If we can achieve a high-performing procurement process then this will be the catalyst that produces high-performance for our company overall.   (Asia-Pacific)

The evidence is that a significant improvement in this process not only achieves direct cost reductions but more powerfully benefits the culture and performance of the business overall. Certainly there are other processes which run right across the business but what is unfortunately different about the procurement process is the lowly status with which it has come to be regarded by business in general. Why this is so is dealt with later. But its being a fact means that to improve attitudes towards it requires near superhuman efforts on the part of those advocating change, and a massive rethinking for the whole corporate team to 'buy in' to the fact that their roles and behaviours may need to change in future. It is the pain involved in the change which makes the cure such a positive and lasting one.

So, procurement is uniquely placed to catalyse the process of culture change in business at the same time as delivering task results of such stunning proportions (some call them quantum leaps or 'breakthroughs') that they change the rules about what is thought to be possible. And part of the culture change is to realise that 'breakthroughs' cannot be forecast by extrapolating previous experience . . . 'best' can only be discovered when we start stretching out for it, and only then by still stretching does best get even better. But why get into the state in the first place such that we have to inflict the pain of rediscovering and reviving the procurement process?

How small businesses get big, and into trouble

Think of the world's best-known companies and many young ones will be on the list – children of their time and with the entrepreneurial parent still much in evidence. But it is noteworthy that the list will contain other enterprises which have been in business for a century or more, and which started small, very small. In them it seems that the two or three founders, although long gone, are still alive. Their picture on the wall is a passive reminder, but their legacy lives on in the form of the vision and core values of business around which they built success – and which are still prized as the founda-tions upon which the modern business is run. In this sense the company can still be held to have the 'young' mindset no matter what its real age. But it is more than the vision and value statements – the true heirs of the entrepreneurs also have a 'feel' for the business and, by having a commercial orientation towards the trading margin, give life to the original meaning of the word 'enterprise'. The feel for the business implies two attributes operating in parallel: an intrinsic ability to handle task or job content in line with customer expectations at the same time as understanding *why* it is being done and feeling about the financial aspects as if it was 'one's own money'. This can be termed 'commercial excellence', or 'commerciality'. Being in a state of perpetual commercial awareness, no matter how intense the task, will mean that the processes going on within the company, and between the company and its customers, suppliers and other external parties, will be both sensed and optimised in order to get the best deals possible and to grow the business. The entrepreneur's mindset can be regarded as the ultimate in 'integration of the total business process'. Embedding the founders' 'genetic code' for the business into modern corporate life forms, which themselves have evolved by experience, virtually guarantees survival of the species, but only for as long as commercial *raison d'être* and competitive advantage remain to the fore. So, what can go wrong?

The problem: business growth by mutation rather than evolution

To start on a positive note, let's look at a 'grown-large' operation which has got its act together (figure 1.1). The central block of the diagram illustrates the company 'asset' – the equipment and people employed in the 'value-adding' process which may be to produce something or to provide service. The picture illustrates how the primary functions interlock to become an integrated value-adding process: procurement creates the high-value low-cost base upon which the operational process (manufacturing or service) can build intrinsic value. Then marketing and sales create and deliver perceived value in the eyes of the ultimate customers.

However, many large operations look like this but do not act like it. The problem is that in the growing-up process the genetic code gets scrambled and the commercial edge dulled. Having started life with temporary help and hired equipment in rented premises the young company, inspired by a cost-saving logic, invests in its first assets. Indeed this could be the first critical fork in the road – investing in new assets to secure a competitive foothold or to grow or expand the business is fine, but to do so merely with the idea of doing the existing job cheaper may be the first step along the road towards an obsession with cost reduction which neglects the need to nurture the business and its key processes. 'I own assets, therefore I am in business' is the attitude which swiftly leads to their becoming a liability. 'I am in business, therefore I need resources and assets (preferably someone else's)' is a better motto in an age when being lean and agile is the precursor of full corporate health.

And so the company grows: staff need supervising, benefits packages and motivation; assets need financing and servicing, and all this needs a management team who, given the operational 'pull' of the task, become preoccupied with managing what the business has become rather than focussing on the vision of what it is there to achieve. Demanding customers claim attention, so it is just as well that, on the supply side, there are suppliers who can meet 'every' demand – albeit at a price! In this way the buyer's role is reduced to one of transmitting increasingly urgent and ill-thought-through needs to the supply market and ensuring that deals have a firm contractual footing. Meanwhile people inside the company become progressively uncertain about what exactly *is* the corporate goal. For the most part they are left with doing what they think is best. This often takes the form of pursuing functional excellence for its own

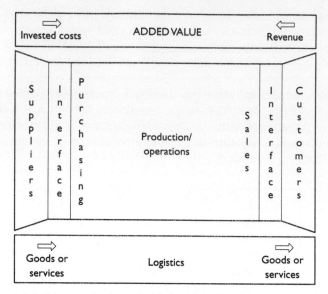

Figure 1.1 Primary roles in maximising added value (*Source*: Russill, 1988)

sake, because no one is asserting other priorities. And far be it for the buyer to challenge what the user wants, after all 'it is the user's budget and his or her money to do with as they wish'. Of course this is an over-simplification but it is, none the less, still worryingly close to the truth for many companies. Perhaps the road to better times leads in the direction of becoming smaller again.

How big businesses get small, and into trouble

Although the seeds of problems may have been sown a while ago evidence of their existence often comes much later, for example when competitors have emerged and are consistently first to seize new market opportunities, or when growing internal costs can no longer be offset by sales price increases or supply cuts. Remedial actions fall under two headings: culture-change and structural, used alone or sometimes together. Again, let's start on a positive note.

Referring again to figure 1.1, both culture-change and structural approaches focus on the size of the central block in order to shed all non-essential activity and then to optimise what is left. Focussing on core-activity means that businesses are contracting out more and more, a trend which is driving total supply-side expenditures (expressed as a percentage of total sales revenue) from traditional mid 50 to high 80 per cent. Other forces in the supply market are leading to the existence of larger suppliers, and fewer of them. Meanwhile, information technology enables data from across the largest conglomerates to be condensed and surveyed. The result is that businesses which are big (in terms of extensive networks, influence and revenues) begin to look small again with fewer owned assets. The challenge for procurement is clear: 'to manage a large part of our company which we do not own, cannot see, and which is staffed by people who we don't employ'. Figure 1.2 illustrates this, and also shows why some gurus are envisioning the future company as a 'switchboard' connecting buyers with sellers whilst being involved only to a minimal extent in the physical processes of adding value.

Culture-change initiatives endeavour to point people towards cross-business processes. Task or functional competence remains vital but not to the extent that business or commercial goals are ignored. The process ethos therefore seeks to get individuals thinking and behaving like 'business-people', and also seeing their jobs as parts of a collaborative team effort. 'Creative commercial collaboration' would seem to be the motto and, if done well, then the reengineering towards effective processes can deliver awesome results in terms of business performance. The key is that attitudes and behaviours have been transformed, not just job contents and work procedures. Figure 1.2 illustrates a highly optimised and perhaps extreme business process with the company no longer overly burdened with managing the internal assets. It is engaging in what amounts to a high-level brokering process. Just like the founding entrepreneur.

But, whilst moving towards this business model is fine, much damage can be inflicted on the way, especially if the change is widespread and only deals with 'structural' issues. This happens when it is not so much the scalpel as the chain-saw which is inflicted on the body corporate, i.e. management seemingly obsessed only with short-term costs and headcount numbers without putting them in the context of a future vision for the business. In their excellent book (Hammer and Champy, 1993) Hammer and Champy describe this futile activity as 'tantamount to rearranging the deck chairs on the Titanic'. And with fewer on the payroll, people do not just become demotivated as tasks are piled on to them but come to feel that they are expendable. The 'company-first' mindset gives way to 'me-first'. Perhaps a company which seems determined to 'sweat the tangible and human assets' is sending a message that the business no longer intends to be a long-term player in that particular business sector and wants, as it were, to cash in the chips. And if that is not the intent, 'outsourcing' and 'down-sizing' the business may nevertheless have irreversibly hollowed out the heart and mind of the business to such an extent that the 're-structuring' actually amounts to 'de-struction'.

Perhaps the answer is to do more for ourselves and aim 'to get big again' – and so the business pendulum gets the push it needs to reverse direction and grow from small to big again. All this expends energy which in terms of company history does little more than pass the time until some future date when the over-heavy body-corporate needs to shed weight again.

Figure 1.2 Big business can look small

■ The best of both worlds

The 'Centrepreneur'

For too long, growing businesses have been increasingly preoccupied with managing what they have become, losing sight of why they started out in business in the first place. Reacting to the immediate problem by aiming to get a bit bigger or a lot smaller will yield temporary relief but will still keep the pendulum swinging. Something more fundamental is needed.

In these businesses the vision, focus, values and drive of the entrepreneur need to be recreated. The challenge is to establish the entrepreneurial processes present in 'start-up' companies but in a structured way appropriate to the scale of large business. This abstract idea is made more relevant, and the chances of successful change increased, if the change strategy is focussed on a tangible aspect of business. The procurement process, itself a microcosm of the business overall, is that candidate for change – both for change to itself and as the catalyst for company-wide transformation towards becoming 'best'. The benefits will be twofold: direct profit or value enhancement and, perhaps the real prize, a transformed corporate culture. These aims can be focussed in one mindset: that of the 'Centrepreneur' (figure 1.3).

Here the vision, energy, agility and creativity of the entrepreneur are allied to the positive aspects of operating within a corporate framework: focus through goal setting and planning, appropriate control, connection with other corporate resources or business entities, and the impact made when the whole is more than the sum of the parts – the best of both worlds.

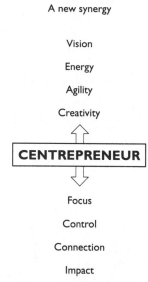

A new synergy

Vision

Energy

Agility

Creativity

⇧

CENTREPRENEUR

⇩

Focus

Control

Connection

Impact

Figure 1.3 The best of both worlds

Procurement Renaissance

Creating companies peopled with 'Centrepreneurs' implies major change for many. Such a programme can be designated as 'Procurement Renaissance'. This is concerned with identifying, selecting and implementing an overall change plan designed to reestablish the procurement process as part of the heart of the business so that it is able to make a maximum contribution to the achievement of corporate goals and, where appropriate, competitive advantage. It is the foundation upon which 'Strategic Procurement' is based. The concept of Strategic Procurement is discussed more fully at the end of chapter 3. Among other factors, Procurement Renaissance includes defining the purpose of the procurement process, the way all people (not just the buyers) work together, their calibre, the policy and operational framework, and the organisational structure which will permit maximum organisational effectiveness.

Why 'Renaissance'? Because if the change is done properly it can transform the culture and capability of the entire corporate team. This is discussed in chapter 8 in the context of, as one company puts it, PreEminent Organisational Effectiveness. Forward-looking companies are now focussing more on why they are in business and as a result are looking hard at what they do, with a view to seeing if they can do just as well 'without it'. Organisational structures are undergoing fundamental change and there are questions about whole departments whose traditional function has gone unchallenged for too long. The aim is to concentrate management's energy on the primary processes which add value to shareholder investment and in the best companies the process of influencing external supply-side resources is one of them. **If Procurement Renaissance is deployed as the means of transforming total effectiveness, then already good companies can become a great deal better.**

■ References

Russill, R. C. (1988), 'Business, logistics and materials management in the nineties – an international survey focussed in a personal opinion'. Proceedings of 'INFOTRANS '88' conference, October, Gothenburg, Sweden.

Hammer, Michael and James Champy (1993), *Reengineering the Corporation, A Manifesto for Business Revolution*, London: Nicholas Brealey.

Chapter two

Core beliefs in a changing business world

Mindsets which can emancipate, or mar, corporate performance

■ Procurement's impact: specialism or profound influence?

Statement: Procurement is poised to make a significant contribution to competitive advantage and business success as we move into the next millennium. **Problem:** This is not a universal perception. Indeed, in many businesses there is not just doubt about the function's contribution, but also open **hostility** to its existence.

There are two key questions: Does procurement make impact just *through the application of specialist knowledge*? Or: Does it *exert a more profound influence* on the key processes at work within a business in its efforts to deliver the results expected by its shareholders and the other bodies to whom it is accountable?

Certainly, in addition to commercial acumen, buyers need enough technical and legal knowledge to deal effectively with day to day needs and to be seen as credible by internal users and suppliers. But to see the contribution simply in terms of specialist input is to forget the origins of business and the importance of supply resources to the entrepreneur, and to be blind to the impact of significant trends in business and in the supply market. These demand a new response from procurement, and in most companies a whole new attitude from the rest of the corporate team.

Changing this attitude, whilst painful, is healthy for businesses seeking to get fit again. But do we have to bother with corporate fitness? If this is your reaction, then the future will be painful – and that's only *if* your company survives in the first place. The world-class players who have set their sights on being around long term (and often have been already) will also bear some pain as they experience the frustration involved in changing company cultures and other people's long-held attitudes to fundamental aspects of business. But they will also taste the excitement of leading their companies towards sustained high performance. As the challenge gets clearer, the smart companies are those who are beginning to see 'procurement' not just as 'profit contributor' able to deliver results to the bottom line better than the diminishing returns from increasing sales or making in-house economies, but also as the 'management tool' for leading the way in revitalising corporate organisational effectiveness overall. The main reason is that the changes required to realise procurement's full potential are also the changes needed to turn lumbering task-oriented organisationally cramped companies into the agile and responsive performers demanded by tomorrow's ever-more dynamic business environment.

The urgency behind these statements derives not just from the specific demands of fast-changing business and supply scenarios, but also from the realisation that what limits the usefulness of breathtaking advancements in technology is not technology and related facilities, but people. The winners will be those companies organising to excel because of their people, the losers will be those trying to win despite them. First, then, a look at the changing supply scenario.

> The winners will be those who are reorganising (or better, *reorchestrating*) attitudes and processes . . . the losers will be marking time redrawing where the lines go to connect boxed-in tasks on the traditional organisation chart.

■ Trends in supply-side exposure

To avoid writing a 'world history of business', the following observations are confined to matters pertinent to the story this book aims to tell, and to put 'today' into perspective. Doing it chronologically is tidy, but business is untidy, meaning that all businesses, supply markets, governments, etc. do not march in step. A key point is that some companies were already doing things in the late 1970s and 1980s which the majority only discovered for themselves in the 1990s. Even more relevant, there are many companies around who put today's date on their letterheads but who are still operating with 1960s/70s cultures and attitudes to business overall and to order-placement's role in particular. One legitimate reason would be that they exist within newly liberated economies (e.g. Eastern Europe) and from this starting point they have the real opportunity to leapfrog the growing phases experienced by businesses elsewhere, and thus quantum jump into a leadership position. Other companies however have attitudes frozen at some point in history. Maybe these coincide with the time when the newly hired senior executives saw their job in terms of managing the business instead of providing leadership for it. They have a lot to do to catch up with, but much to gain from, the modern approach.

1960/70s: Competing for growth

Business:
- relatively easy profits
- business success hides internal inefficiencies
- long product life-cycles

Supply side:
- buyers highly product-oriented: need for technical expertise
- buyers focus on serving the user: reactive image
- many sources: available and used
- sellers seeking buyers

- adversarial, arm's-length relationships
- buyers threatening to 'take business elsewhere', but buying procedures reflect trust in the supply market

1980s: Competing for cost reduction

Business:
- shorter product life-cycles
- squeeze on profits, pressure on costs
- focus on 'quality of work' to improve company efficiency and effectiveness
- growing dependence on 'systems' to improve efficiencies
- increasing decentralisation to create autonomous business units

Supply side:
- procurement beginning to be seen as pro-active and a profit contributor
- need to reduce stocks . . . supplier performance improvement a key priority
- focus on supply chain management to remove wasted supply costs
- consolidation of volumes to leverage better deals
- fewer, larger suppliers
- buyers seeking sellers for new products/lower costs
- closer, more focussed supplier relationships, although policies and procedures reflect that the buyer is trusted more than the market overall

1990s: Competing for hearts and minds

Business:
- dramatically increasing international competition
- fast-emerging new markets and new economies
- rapid change: technological, structural, externally imposed constraints
- businesses envisaging 'being the best in their business'
- more visibility between companies via 'benchmarking' activities
- wider adoption of matrix management with people holding multiple responsibilities
- big businesses transforming themselves into 'federations of small ones'
- decentralisation now includes 'strategic alliances' and 'distributed companies', but business 'globalisation' reawakens centralist themes
- focus on process re-engineering to enhance effectiveness
- trend to outsource all but core activity but increasing question of what *is* 'core activity'!
- greater exposure to third parties

Supply side:
- emphasis on 'providing customer response' sharpens role of logistics
- more examples of use of 'buying consortia' to increase leverage

- procurement role to create high-value, high-performance, low-cost supply base
- procurement emphasis on managing external (*and* internal) relationships
- supply chains becoming supply networks with customer influence over them extending up the supplier's own supply chain
- joint customer–supplier technology development activity
- procurement and sourcing management perspectives increasingly visible in business and management debate, with commensurate increase in development of new concepts and fashions
- clear evidence of strategic procurement planning and action playing major roles in companies achieving 'results breakthroughs'

2000+? Survival through revival

Business:
- quantum light-speed change: 'I blinked for a moment – which way did it go?'
- competitive edge means not having a permanent differentiator, but being able to innovate, operate, anticipate and capture opportunities faster than the competition – permanently
- information flowing at light speed down optic super-highways – decisions needing to be made 'at the speed of light'
- 'Being best' now defined in terms of the culture and inherent organisational effectiveness at producing stupendous results and going on getting better, rather than in terms of the results themselves
- company organisations not confining people to 'cells in the managed matrix', but instead creating space in which they can perform
- global 'open world' visibility

Supply side:
- procurement now seen as 'acquisition management'
- elimination of permanent procurement departments, with key decisions and actions being taken by 'transient work teams' forming up and disbanding under the overall leadership of the corporate commercial process 'conductor'
- a company's customer-satisfaction process (in product terms) will primarily be lead by the equivalent of today's key customer account manager, whereas the company's commercial process (in terms of margin optimisation, and assuming that internal activities are by now cost-optimised following reengineering initiatives) will hinge on successfully dealing with the customer's buyers, and on 'our' procurement process successfully dealing with supplier's sellers

Procurement: its critical importance

Well, we can all hypothesise about the future and table 2.1 provides space for your views! But, in terms of past and present, the changing scenario outlined above shows

Table 2.1 Characteristics of 2000+

	Your views
Business	
Supply side	

a dramatic evolution in the prominence of procurement activity. Hardly surprising since this book is dedicated to the subject. But more important is that this story is dedicated not to some narrow functionalism but to the achievement of very best business results, and it is increasingly the fact that the best companies are seeing procurement as the means of achieving them. Here are the five 'core beliefs' which make high-class companies now see procurement change as a primary force capable of driving a company towards achieving its vision of being 'best' in future.

■ Five core beliefs

1. The success of many companies increasingly depends on securing access to the best suppliers – suppliers who are committed and able to perform to the highest level and who see the buyer's company as a premier customer.
2. Best value for money in acquiring materials and services is only realised when a highly professional and dedicated procurement capability exists, working through a multi-specialist cross-business procurement process, characterised by close collaboration with business managers and task specialists and comprising people who are empowered to work in a way which achieves their full personal potential. Note that this does not necessarily mean the existence of a procurement organisation in the form of the traditional department. What is needed is an organised approach to procurement: quite different.
3. A consistent image and approach is essential in all interactions between the customer company and its external supply environment . . . locally and globally. Without this there is fragmentation and the certainty of lost commercial advantage.
4. Strategic planning tools and techniques, backed up by specialist systems and controls, are required to ensure that the acquisition of services, materials and knowledge is conducted in the most effective way within the framework of corporate controls and accountability, and at the same time complies with the legal, political and ethical expectations of the community at large.

5. The acquisition or procurement 'process' is one of the primary value-adding business activities which leads to satisfaction of shareholders' expectations of the company. (In the public sector one aspect of this is achieving best value for money; in private business, making profit.) Changes which create a high-performing procurement process provide the catalyst for achieving corporate excellence overall, and as such provide a unique opportunity for procurement to provide the lead which upgrades company performance to become 'best'.

A more direct message

We may need suppliers more than they need us.

Company in-fighting and chaotic expenditure costs money.

The external supply environment is a jungle.

Procurement is not a mechanistic activity: there IS science and strategy in it.

No longer can users behave like prima donnas: only a process of focussed teamwork delivers best performance.

■ The 'core beliefs' examined in detail

First to have access . . .

The success of many companies increasingly depends on securing access to the best suppliers . . . suppliers who are committed and able to perform to the highest level and who see the buyer's company as a premier customer.

We start with the bad news. Poor supplier performance costs the customer money. One company calculates that the effect of poor performance is to increase costs by 10–15 per cent. Going on from this, sophisticated manufacturing techniques have demanded that suppliers' performance rate highly on efficiency, reliability and cost effectiveness, and buyers are increasingly aware that excellence in these areas has to be achieved in a collaborative manner rather than crudely demanded. Many companies are therefore implementing strategies to get closer to fewer suppliers, but this means the customer company ends up with 'more eggs in fewer baskets'. Managing external *relationships* therefore becomes the priority, a shift from order-placement's traditional emphasis on optimising individual *transactions*. In addition, the familiar advice to 'focus on core activity' is achieving new significance as companies contract out business functions which have until recently remained in-house – to the extent that as much as 85 per cent of incoming sales revenue may now be being committed as expenditure in the supply market. Managing and motivating these external resources is critical for business success and it becomes more appropriate to define the buyer's role as 'managing a large part of our company which we do not own, cannot see, and which is staffed by people who we don't employ'.

So far, then, it seems that it is the buyer who is in the position of being able to call the shots; *but we also need to persuade key suppliers to stay with us*. Why is this? Surely in this age of customer focus they should be able to motivate themselves? Though many advocate close collaboration with selected suppliers there are still the die-hards who believe it is up to the supplier to compete and initiate new ideas whilst the buyer waits 'to be delighted'. Reality says otherwise. Supply companies are becoming more choosy about who they wish to sell to. This may be because the customer's needs no longer fit with the supplier's long-term strategy. More often it is because the customer has become too undesirable a proposition: costly to service because of a track record of bad payment, poor forecasting of needs, constantly changing requirements, and so on. Most suppliers enjoy a demanding customer, but only if it provides the positive 'stretch' which challenges the supplier to scale new heights.

So buyers have to inspire the best performance from the best suppliers and, even more difficult, keep suppliers in a ready-to-respond mindset even when an order is not immediately in the offing. Amongst other activities, this involves 'selling' the benefits of the customer company to the supplier, a concept called Procurement Marketing. Without Procurement Marketing, today's successful companies may well become less so in future, exposed to insecure supply sources or losing competitive advantage because another customer is seen as the supplier's first priority.

In many companies, procurement's importance to the business is assumed to be proportional to the size of total expenditure made. 'We are in business therefore we incur costs – the bigger they are the more we need procurement to manage it.' The above comments dispel this assumption. This is because the story is not about price, but about the quality of responses obtained from the supply market and the securing of sources critical to the success of our business. 'Because we are able to trade productively with quality suppliers and have anchored key sources to our cause, then we are enabled to be in business and to meet the goals expected by our shareholders.' Procurement's importance to the business is inherent in being in business in the first place. The size of the total expenditure merely impacts on the numbers of people who need to be engaged directly in managing that activity. But let us look at the cost-management aspect of it, the subject of the next 'core belief'.

Two aspects of internal teamwork

Best value for money in acquiring materials and services is only realised when a highly professional and dedicated procurement capability exists, working through a multi-specialist cross-business procurement process characterised by close collaboration with business managers and functional specialists and which comprises people who are empowered to work in a way which achieves their full personal potential.

The two themes underlying this premise are that '*skilful approaches are required to secure best deals in total cost terms*', and that this is also dependent on '*cross-functional and cross-business collaboration*' throughout the procurement process, from the earliest stages of needs-identification to contract placement.

Skilful approaches

With total corporate supply-side expenditures as high as 85 per cent of incoming revenues in some companies – and even if they are as 'low' as 30 per cent – they provide a major opportunity for profit contribution because of the sheer size of the savings that can be made by imaginative 'eyes open' strategic approaches to the market and also because such savings feed directly through to the bottom line. Strategic planning, building leverage through consolidating requirements, creating competitive dynamics in the supply market – all can deliver 30–40 per cent cost savings on specific deals if the current cost-base is not optimised.

But getting the sums right is only part of the story. There is also the need to be able to read the market trends, look for signs of problems before they materialise as such, and to outmanoeuvre market distortions. The fact that the world is opening up politically, geographically and logistically may make it easier for buyers and sellers to enter new markets, but does not necessarily mean that buyers will enjoy keenly competitive pricing. Economies and markets become more interdependent and major companies straddle the globe. Strategic alliances, take-overs and mergers all contribute to a concentration of sources. Despite the regulations, one may expect a growth in cartels, and these are becoming increasingly clever at disguising their existence. Worse from the buyer's viewpoint, the concentration of sources may mean a large supplier achieving a position where they can allocate supplies, let alone dictate prices. So the price jungle gets thicker. Traditional buyers suffering from 'go for lowest price' myopia may be drawn into an over-dependence on one source, but higher prices will then follow as a monopoly supplier exploits leverage or as cartel members allocate the business. Whatever laws prevail, the reality will be fashioned by corporate entrepreneurs: those with an eye for an opportunity or a loophole. Whilst 'proactive' buyers get ahead of their slower colleagues in anticipating events, tomorrow's new breed buyers will show 'deterministic' behaviour aimed at influencing and shaping their supply market environment rather than accepting it the way it is.

Multi-specialist, cross-business teamwork

The buyer's role in future: what is it?

To bring together the different specialist resources needed to make decisions about the type of supply market which needs to exist to enable the company to be successful now and in future . . . then to take the actions necessary to make that vision become reality.

This is about knowledge, commitment and behaviour, and of these three, the latter is what ultimately matters since it is through the right behaviour that knowledge and commitment are transmitted. The common experience is that bringing different functions together adds significantly to the quality of the work being done. For example in practice when planning strategically for critical acquisitions, it becomes evident that no one person has the whole picture. Technical advice is needed for opinions about the acceptability of different specifications, marketing will assess the impact of that on customer preferences; the buyer may well be providing the driving force for change if he or she sees that supply market trends are posing new threats to the business; and finance will be able to quantify the extent to which profit margin is exposed to adverse supply-side phenomena. But all parties need to be committed to any change proposed, and experience shows that multi-specialist involvement from the start is the prerequisite for wholehearted support when it is time for action.

How multi-specialist, cross-business teamwork is conducted will be discussed in chapters 7 and 8. Meanwhile there is a more urgent issue: how to stop money haemorrhaging out of the company now because of unenlightened behaviour on the part of several different players involved in the procurement process. Most efforts to reduce supply-side costs start at the time when a supplier or contractor has been selected to do the work. Undoubtedly much can be achieved when buyer and seller work together to understand and then reduce costs. Reducing inventory costs by better forecasting of demand and improved delivery accuracy is one example. But the uncomfortable fact is that this work may only be removing costs which *should never be there in the first place* – costs which have been allowed into the equation because of inefficiencies in the early stages of the procurement process. Cost management is therefore an active issue from the time that 'needs' are first thought of, not just a subject awaiting analysis once the customer is committed.

How we can get it wrong is analysed in more detail in the supply chain cost-development curves. Figures 2.1 and 2.2 illustrate this, the good and the bad. Figure 2.1 tracks a good 'base' curve. The internal user's need is identified and the cost of satisfying it may then be reduced by optimising the specification. This cost may then become the budget available to be spent. Now it's over to procurement whose approach to the supply market, plus ensuing negotiations, succeeds in delivering cost savings against budget. The supplier then performs and delivers according to expectations, and the final checks and controls confirm that all is correct and the contractual price can be paid.

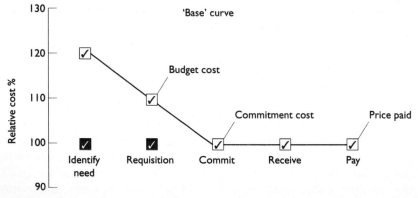

Figure 2.1 A supply chain cost-development curve – good news

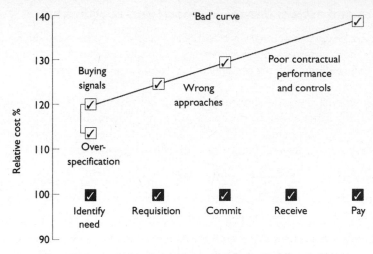

Figure 2.2 A supply chain cost-development curve – bad news

Figure 2.2 is bad news. From the outset, costs are destined to increase. A 'gold-plate' over-specification starts this process. Early technical discussions with possible suppliers unwittingly reveal the customer's buying intentions and perhaps the budgets available. These are examples of 'commercial exposure' which exist during the early phase of the procurement process when it is often assumed that only non-commercial issues are in play. But more is to come. The visible commercial stage, between requisition and commitment, brings new cost-increase threats. Rigid and predictable order-placement tactics; a failure to recognise and get round cartels and monopolies; an over-emphasis on price rather than total cost – these can *add* quantum-leap costs to the customer's bill. Cases can be cited where costs are now 40–50 per cent higher, at the point of commitment, than they are in a figure 2.1 scenario. Let's assume that the contract documents are in order from the legal point of view and so there is no 'legal exposure'. However, costs may be set to increase further through the cost of poor supplier performance, claims and changes to what was ordered, and uncontrolled acceptance of price increases. These illustrate 'contractual exposure'. A curve 2 scenario sounds unlikely but unfortunately is all too often encountered in companies where the order-placement effort is under-powered and positioned as a mechanistic support activity: 'ink-stained clerks living in basement cubicles'! (*Fortune*, 20 February 1995).

Chapter 5 describes what a 'best' curve can look like but the point to leave in play at the moment is that supply-side management is not just concerned with 'what' comes down the supply pipeline but is also to do with managing relationships with the people at its source, and the relationship between them and our people. Enlightened behaviour and collaboration throughout this process are a 'must' if wasted effort and wasted cost are to be avoided. Best value equates with best behaviour.

Three-pronged action: image, approach and coordination

A consistent image and approach is essential in all interactions between the customer company and its external supply environment . . . locally and globally. Without this there is fragmentation and the certainty of lost commercial advantage.

Figure 2.2 demonstrated the consequence of uncoordinated effort between different functions on the same site or in the same company. The problem is magnified where there are different companies within the same group but operating as independent entities, maybe across several countries. This allows suppliers to play one part of the customer company off against another. The bottom line is a *damaged* bottom line through loss of leverage. This is because the supply-side expenditure is spread too thinly across too many suppliers, but internal costs soar due to the heavy administration costs of dealing with so many different sources.

The corporate Procurement Vice-President of a global pharmaceutical company was touring the company's operating locations and, in the course of each site visit, asked how much laboratory equipment was purchased for that site from a certain (also global) equipment supplier. The accumulated picture was more than anyone had thought. Next stop? . . . a visit to the sales chief of the equipment company. Our V.P. laid out the facts. 'Gee, I hate it when our customers get their act together', admitted the sales supremo before getting down to business to agree a deal very much to the benefit of the customer.

Table 2.2 illustrates the spread of supplier allegiance in one global company. The data were gleaned from 15 companies within the same group, each listing their top 20 suppliers by spend. Two hundred and eight suppliers were named but in no case was any supplier identified as common to all locations. The best situation was one supplier common to ten locations, yet the suppliers named are all global players. This represents a serious fragmentation of leverage, but to correct it does not necessarily mean that different sites have to buy from the same supplier. The key is to have a common global strategy within which relationships with key suppliers are maximised but which leave room for local opportunities which fit within the overall strategy.

Consolidating on key sources can deliver significant internal and external cost savings, but there remains the larger question of credibility and attractiveness as a

Table 2.2 Spread of supplier allegiance

No. of locations	Common suppliers
10	1
7	2
6	3
4	3
3	8
2	11
No commonality	108

customer. Both are enhanced if it is clear to the outside world that the company's left hand knows what the right is doing. But, more critically, each individual company may look like a small fish to a big supplier with the result that each is downgraded to being less than a premium customer. The real benefit in getting the act together could be to achieve being repositioned as a key, strategic customer deserving of a very different response from the supplier in terms of receiving preferential treatment and innovation, not merely lower prices.

So, in a world where supply companies often have a better view of the big picture than does a large but fragmented customer, it is necessary to coordinate to even up the balance of leverage. But does this mean that all companies aiming to be successful in well-integrated supply markets should conduct procurement activity through a centralised office? Again a dilemma – how best to maximise overall impact at a time when company operations may extend over a wide geographical area and indeed the company itself may be reorganising or newly reshaped into autonomous business units? Whilst decentralising procurement and other business functions is in vogue for some companies, there are the problems of fragmentation described above, plus another minus: fragile reporting lines back to the centre and in bad cases the tendency for business units to 'declare independence'. And as time passes some once-slim decentralised businesses start getting fat, leading to a cry for centralising as the means of slimming down and capturing the economies of scale. Some companies spend their lives oscillating between the two extremes, exhausting their energies which should otherwise be devoted to beating the competition. Is there an alternative? There is, and it is called the CLAN approach – the Centre-Led Action Network. This, described in chapter 7, is most definitely not a compromise between the two extremes of the organisational pendulum, but a structure having its own identity, and able to make a profound impact on the way businesses must organise themselves to survive and succeed in the next millennium.

Four pillars: tools, techniques, systems and controls

Strategic planning tools and techniques, backed up by specialist systems and controls, are required to ensure that the acquisition of services, materials and knowledge is conducted in the most effective way within the framework of corporate controls and accountability . . . and at the same time complying with the legal, political and ethical expectations of the community at large.

This is about the infrastructure which supports procurement activity. A typical company makes extensive expenditures in the supply market, and because it means 'going outside' it is also a very public business. It's not just that political or public relations issues attend major contract placement but, in line with best business practice, the processes involved need to be robust, able to withstand scrutiny and to meet modern expectations as regards corporate governance. This requires the customer company to have clear policies in place which apply to all concerned with the procurement process – and 'all' involves not just the buyers but also the CEO and most others in the company who influence the process by their authorities and their behaviours. Then there needs to be objectivity and structure in the key decision-making processes. Once, the 'back of the envelope' sufficed. Now, the best-practice players are calling into play a wide range of decision-making techniques and strategy-planning tools which bring sophistication and science into the early stages of acquisition planning. Without them prejudices and assumptions go unchallenged, and data-bytes stay as data without becoming 'intelligence'. With them the multi-specialist cross-business teams have the means by which they can be architects of winning supply-market strategies. Without them, well, 'we make it up as we go along' – hardly a sensible use of hard-earned sales revenue.

A fifth dimension: the value of process

> The acquisition or procurement 'process' is one of the primary value-adding business activities which leads to satisfaction of shareholders' expectations of the company. (In the public sector one aspect of this is achieving best value for money; in private business, making profit.) Changes which create a high-performing procurement process provide the catalyst for achieving corporate excellence overall, and as such provide a unique opportunity for procurement to provide the lead which upgrades company performance to become 'best'.

First, another short history of business. Consider the entrepreneur at the outset. Having 'nothing' of their own in terms of assets they see an opportunity in the supply market, buy in to it and sell on at a profit, if necessary creating customer interest such that they want to buy at the price proposed. The same may happen in reverse. Either way, business is about watching and influencing the interface between 'inputs' and 'outputs', and succeeding at the cash-balancing act so that positive profit and cash flows result. Being successful, the company grows. Some companies, like 'resellers', always stay looking like their entrepreneurial origins – a few people at the centre bringing a network of suppliers into touch with a network of customers. But all growing companies encounter a fork in the road when the priorities can subtly and dangerously change – when it's not 'making the business' but 'running the business' which becomes the preoccupation of senior management. On top of this they may decide to invest in assets of their own instead of using others'. Asset-management issues now arise; manufacturing expertise may begin to develop. Now the danger is that top management have become preoccupied with 'managing what the business has become' rather than remembering *why* they are in business in the first place. Functions grow, departmental turf battles break out. The energy which the owner/founder brought to the business is now dissipated internally, and the once-clear focus blurred. 'We fly aeroplanes because we are an airline . . . pity we have to have passengers' is a mindset which has brought some major companies close to going under, whether airlines or not. The stage is set for dramatic change. A predator may take them over to strip out the assets, including the people, to increase efficiencies. Or the company itself may pre-empt that trauma by initiating the change process itself. Either way, the change will be painful.

What's this got to do with procurement? Two things.

The first is to emphasise that suppliers are an essential ingredient to business success, being the foundation upon which business was built in the first place. To ignore that is like trying to make fire without fuel. The procurement process is thus an integral part of the value-creation chain and its role statement needs to reflect this.

> To provide a high-value, low-cost supply base upon which the company can be successful in achieving its business objectives both now and in future . . . and to secure that position by actively managing the company's exposure to the supply market and to competitor activity within it.

The second point concerns the widespread but low-level perceptions of the procurement process, and its cross-functional nature. This point was made in chapter 1 and is expanded at the end of chapter 6.

■ A new 'investment opportunity'

The finance community have a lot to answer for! Figures presented in company Profit and Loss (P&L) statements are usually sufficiently broad that they can be used to convey whatever message one wants. Whilst the generalisations forced on the data by the accounting conventions may be necessary in order to put vastly different businesses on to a comparable footing, the problem is that some key aspects of business dynamics become hidden in the process, particularly the distinction between 'revenue' and 'cost'. Terms like 'cost' and 'expenditure' have an unfortunately negative ring about them and suggest that 'revenue' is not just a good thing but would be a deal better if costs had not pushed in to spoil things. An Operations Director of a grocery company is properly turned on to the value of the supply side of business. But he also says: 'I hate costs . . . I think it's a good thing to hate costs.' The target of his venom is not costs per se but, quite rightly, wasted costs. *Wasted* costs do push profit under, whereas what we might call *invested* costs actually *pull* forward the resources needed for the business to be in business in the first place.

Positive costs

The idea of making revenue without investing in 'positive costs' at the supply side belongs to the mindset that expects to earn interest on an investment without first putting up any capital. Or as one European agent for a US company observed: 'You know what they're like: they want to earn the profit before they've made and sold the product!'. Sure, investment-free enterprise becomes possible if the customer pays up-front and the suppliers (not to mention one's own staff) are happy to wait for payment in future, but this requires active persuasion at both ends of the business if it's going to work.

The other problem with the normal P&L statement is that the sheer scale of 'supply-side' investment is concealed within the larger number entered under 'costs of sales' or 'operating expenses'. The consequence of all this is that supply-side costs neither have the 'feel good' factor nor do they register in total terms as belonging in the same league as incoming revenues.

The Introduction, question 1, showed a P&L statement of a manufacturing company trading (as a network of some seven smaller companies) across Europe. The incoming revenue of '100' is scaled down from real life, but the other figures are in their correct ratios. The newly appointed Group Procurement Manager decided that they could be shown differently, as in table 2.3. The result usefully augmented his campaign to change attitudes to the procurement process as one of the key value creation activities within the business. It also revealed the true scale of the supply-side exposure of the business.

Table 2.3 P&L statement

	$ million as %
Sales revenue	100.0
Supply market spend	(64.8)
Gross margin	35.2
Costs of adding value	(22.0)
Net margin	13.2
Tax/interest, etc.	(5.9)
Trading profit	7.3

Figure 2.3 shows the supplier–company–customer model and depicts 'income and investment flows' as per the dialogue above. We do not want the business world to change its terminology – just its attitudes to 'positive costs', be they invested internally in human resources and capital assets or externally to pull forward responses and resources from the external supply market. And we want the people in the company who are 'outside' procurement to recognise that, whilst the mechanics of raising requisitions and committing to contracts may involve relatively few players at the trading interface, the involvement of many in both companies is essential if best deals are to be created.

■ Summary

There is unmistakable evidence now that today's excellent companies are looking at their 'cost investment' in the supply market in a positive way, not just as a source of significant cost-reduction potential, but also as a means of 'buying in' to the creativity and motivation of external companies who may happen to be the best available in understanding and providing what it is the customer really needs. Spending money is not a necessary evil as a result of being in business; investing money in the right way with the right suppliers is the prerequisite for being successfully in business in the

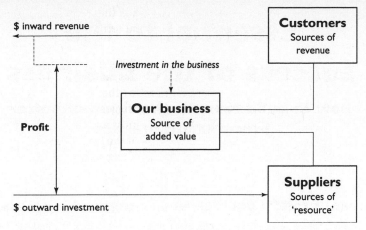

Figure 2.3 How the procurement process fits into the business model

first place. Acceptance that supply-side expenditures can be positive costs opens up fundamentally new opportunities.

The five core beliefs represent both the feelings and facts about what is important in business today. But laying out the facts alone seldom wins people's hearts and minds. Their own perceptions and prejudices get in the way and, even if the logic is privately accepted, public resistance is needed in order to save face. So it is as important to know not just *what* the story is about (i.e. the core beliefs) but also *how* to tell it. This is dealt with in chapter 3.

■ Reference

'Order-placement's new muscle', *Fortune*, 20 February 1995.

Chapter three

Essential to the success of the business

How to build towards the vision of better procurement practice

■ Procurement's role: if you believe . . . no proof is necessary

There's a biblical story about the waters of the Red Sea parting to create a dry passageway for a crowd of people to cross safely and thus escape from their pursuers. Scientists now calculate that it is physically possible that this happened. All that was needed was the right combination of tides and wind conditions. But 'believers' have faith that it was a miracle. A recent discussion on this topic ended with this phrase: 'for those who *don't* believe, no proof is possible . . . but for those who *do*, no proof is necessary'.

Back in today's world, this last comment says a lot about the challenge facing buyers in getting the message across about procurement's contribution to the business. Buyers have to get users and senior management to *believe* in the need for professional procurement – and spend less time measuring and comparing questionable statistics to justify their existence.

Changing the mindset is a formidable challenge. We have already seen how small-business chiefs value their supply sources whereas many corporate executives tend to see order-placement as an undesirable consequence of being in business. What is more, they think, it is 'easy' to do and does not require the best people to be put on the job. What factors account for this latter attitude? Here are some commonly made assumptions which explain why:

■ that the supply market is genuinely competitive . . . always
■ that prices are based on costs . . . always
■ that pushing for lower prices endangers quality . . . always
■ that suppliers are anxious to do 'almost anything' to please their customers . . . always
■ that it is logical that, since the customer has the money that the supplier wants, the buyer has the stronger position

Assumptions like these lead to the view that buying is easy and that the best deals are to be found simply by exercising the formalities of inviting suppliers to compete for the business. For as long as customers believe this, the supplier enjoys the advantage. Why? Because they:

- can predict the buyer's game plan
- know that if they can 'sell' the user and/or senior management on the benefits of the deal, then commercial considerations take a back seat
- can collude with each other if they have a mind to

But even this simple logic fails to convince many non-buyers in the company. This is because the use of logic, even though it can be successful in 'proving a case', will seldom shift long-held attitudes and perceptions – especially if the other party does not want to change their position. Some may feel threatened by the logic, the more so if they feel that to give 'procurement' a higher priority will actually limit their own decision-making freedoms. Others are basing their position on the world they knew yesterday, when they may even have done some buying, and have lost touch with today's reality.

To be successful in selling the message needs attention to both content and process. *What* that message is, and *how* it is communicated are two separate issues. Its content simply stated is: a high-class procurement process contributes directly to profit and competitive advantage, can generate cash, optimises external exposure and ensures legality and accountability. This is a powerful message, being a mixture of logic (profit from cost saving, cash generation, etc.) and fear (the consequences of over-exposure). But although these facts are obvious to many, perceptions of procurement's role still remain unsatisfactory. This is because facts seldom speak for themselves, especially if the other party is determined to remain deaf to them. 'Selling the vision' is a separate challenge. The aim is to make collaboration during the procurement process an irresistible idea to others. A lot depends on their perceptions and attitudes right now. This is the place to start. Don't go too quickly for the big vision because it will seem too far off to be credible and achievable.

Here is a stepwise approach to building up people's perception of what it is all about. What is needed is to decide which 'step' your listener is on at the moment and then talk them up to the next one.

Stairway to the process vision

If they think procurement's unnecessary . . . the message is 'standards and control'

Produce data which show just how much money is being spent in the supply market by your company.

> *How does the sales revenue income get spent in one company?*
> 13 per cent is profit before tax; 28 per cent are costs including taxes, depreciation, staff costs, etc.; and 59 per cent is spent with third parties on all the supplies and services needed to enable the company to be in business and to grow. The 59 per cent equates to an expenditure of $5 million per day. Expressing the figures like this jolted the Board into giving new support to procurement.

The above shows the situation in an international company in the 'household consumable products' business. Answering the question this way, illustrating the figures as a pie-chart, revealed the true extent of supply-side expenditure. And yet, before these figures were revealed in this way, the expenditure activity was regarded as clerical work. Expenditure in the 50–60 per cent range is fairly typical of many manufacturing companies although it is growing as companies increasingly outsource all but core activity. High-tech electronic companies and re-seller operations are cases in point where expenditures can be 80–90 per cent of sales income.

Other comparisons reveal inconsistencies in the way many top-management teams allocate their time when addressing cost-reduction issues. For example, there is a limit to how much more can be saved by putting further pressure on reducing people-numbers, which may account for only 10–12 per cent of the above 28 per cent. Yet this remains a major management obsession. And although costs approximately six times bigger, and a huge cost-saving potential, exist at the supply side of the business, it can still be difficult to get procurement on to the boardroom agenda.

In some companies the lack of systems is such that no one is sure how much is being spent with which suppliers, and by whom. Is this the way to squander hard-earned income or budgets? Hardly a way to impress the shareholders. It's also likely that contractual safeguards are non-existent and, worse still, a contract entered into by a 'buyer' not possessing the legal authority may be deemed an invalid contract in a court of law. So, a story built around the statistics and dimensions of expenditure activity, spiced with examples of scurrilous suppliers taking advantage of weak or unsound contracts, may at least get minds open to the existence of major exposures at the supply side of the business and the need for expenditures to be properly controlled and risk managed.

If they see procurement as regulator of the order-placement process . . . the message is 'prices are not fixed'

Many executives seem to believe that purchase prices are inevitable, a direct consequence of manufacturing costs and raw material or component supply prices, and that there is not much that can be done about them. Many prices are calculated in this way. Yet a cost-plus pricing policy is only one of many different pricing policies that a seller can use to achieve specific objectives. Knowing more about sellers' pricing, stopping 'buying signals' and having ambitious targets can lead to significant price reductions compared with the seller's opening offer. And if our minds are fixed on the idea that prices are always based on costs, then we are conditioned to expect always to have to pay for something and are consequently blinded to other opportunities.

The message is: *everything about price is negotiable* – and don't be fooled into thinking that once the need has been specified the price automatically follows from the cost-plus calculation. Any one company (the buyer's own, even) may have as many different prices for the same product as they have customers for it. So, as well as bringing control into the expenditure process, buyers can put pressure on price rather than meekly accepting what is offered.

A small company in Thailand recently acquired a complete closed-circuit television surveillance system to protect it's premises . . . for free, and from a willing supplier. During negotiations it came out that, although they had a good reputation and many customers in other countries, this would be the supplier's first installation of this equipment in Thailand – and they wanted to expand into that market. The buyer successfully proposed that the equipment should be installed for nil cost, in which case the customer would be happy to allow the supplier to bring other prospective customers to view the set-up in future. 'But', added the buyer to the salesperson, 'it would be embarrassing, wouldn't it, if your visitors came on a day when the equipment may not be working properly . . .' The salesperson took the hint and added free maintenance into the deal. Win–win!

If they see procurement as about achieving lowest price . . . talk about 'profit contribution'

It is more common now for people to be talking about total acquisition cost, or total lifetime cost. This accounts for the fact that the total cost paid today is more than just the price asked. Non-price factors (e.g. delivery, payment terms, etc.) add to the total actually paid. Then additional costs during the life of the item purchased (e.g. maintenance, or operational inefficiency) contribute to lifetime costs being larger than initial costs. Show how skilful procurement can improve margins by saving on total lifetime costs in a number of creative, and often dramatic, ways and show that these savings flow directly to bottom-line profitability. End of lifetime disposal costs can also be bigger because of environmental constraints, and come quicker because of earlier technical obsolescence.

A business newspaper provided a recent illustration that managing margins, not boosting sales, is the better way to improve profitability, especially in a post-recession period when it is tempting to grab any new orders which come along.

Table 3.1 shows how a margin improvement achieved by cutting costs by 1 per cent, or by putting up prices 1 per cent, can produce a 9–10 per cent profit gain. However, increasing sales creates only a 5 per cent improvement. In addition the latter tactic

Table 3.1 A direct contribution to profit

	Basis	1% cost cut	1% price rise	1% sales rise
Sales income	100	100	101	101
Variable costs	50	49.5*	50	50.5
Fixed costs	40	39.6*	40	40
Net profit	10	10.9	11	10.5

Note: *Reduction of variable costs by striking better deals with suppliers, and fixed cost reductions by outsourcing activity which is not core to the business plus improvements to the effectiveness of procurement process. These comments merely illustrate how cost reductions can be achieved – in practice, actual cost savings are significantly more and can represent a quantum leap from what previously was thought to be possible.

heavily depends on there being enough new customers out there who are willing to buy. But why not do it all? It is interesting that we have become accustomed to thinking that customers can be influenced by skilful marketing and sales approaches (and so that is where our management efforts are focussed) but that the supply market cannot. The reality is otherwise and to apply our best management talent now to the input side of the business can produce significant competitive advantage at a time when the vast majority of companies are still stuck in the order-placement time warp of seeing it merely as an administrative drain on resources.

If it's 'only' about profit contribution . . . demonstrate procurement's 'contribution to other task results'

A sure sign that a company is moving in the right direction as regards the priority given to managing the input side of its business is the existence of a role or mission statement for the procurement activity, and that this talks in terms of profit contributions coming from cost savings. But it's surprising how many enlightened companies' thinking stops here.

In part this is due to the view that procurement is only about optimising individual transactions rather than, more significantly, about managing external relationships. A collaborative effort by buyer and seller jointly searching for cost reduction ideas once a deal has been set up can often yield far more savings than can negotiation on price, no matter how skilfully conducted. But another relationship issue opens up when we challenge the assumption that there's always a supplier out there who wants to supply. Demonstrate the risk-potential to your company should a critical supplier delay or even stop supplying, and develop contingency plans to reduce your exposure to that risk. Look at what other customer companies are calling for from the supply market – any potential shortage will hurt them and not you if you are the customer who has made forward plans to keep your business needs satisfied. If left to themselves, market forces in general will tend to damage your company's chance of being totally successful, and the contribution that procurement can make to protecting and maximising that success will far outweigh what can be done by focussing only on cost-optimising individual deals.

One approach successfully used first in one country within a multi-national petrochemical company was to adapt the methodology usually used in Force-Field Analysis to illustrate the hostile forces conspiring to push a major capital project off schedule and over budget.

Table 3.2 shows the potential failure factors. The same concept, illustrated in table 3.3, was then applied to the positive factors which could enhance project-management's performance.

Project managers tend to have notoriously closed mindsets towards buyers, yet the above approach, being a subtle mix of logic and threat, was successful in opening up a whole new perception for them. This resulted not just in the assignment of high-quality buyers to the project team, but also early involvement of buyers in the early stages of the procurement process when project strategies and targets were being set.

Table 3.2 Potential failure factors

Failure <———————— ¦ ————————> Success
<——————¦—— Rising inflation
<——————¦—— Materials or labour shortage
<——————¦— Suppliers merging or being acquired
<——————¦—— Supplier bankruptcy
<——————¦—— Supplier's resources over-loaded
<——————¦—— Production stoppage or labour disputes
<——————¦—— Equipment becomes obsolete
<——————¦— Design or specification changes
<——————¦— Currency fluctuations
<——————¦— Start-up date advancement
<——————¦—— Transportation limitations
<——————¦—— Shipment delays or demurrage
<——————¦— Legislation changes
<——————¦—— Suppliers' adversarial ploys (e.g. cartels)
<——————¦—— Others

Note: The dashed vertical line represents the initially desired outcome (e.g. project on budget or on-schedule completion); the solid vertical line represents the failed outcome if the hostile external forces were *not* anticipated and managed.

Table 3.2 Potential success factors

Failure <———————— ¦ ————————> Success
Alternative, better, suppliers ———————¦————————>
Substituted, better, cheaper materials ——¦————————>
Global sourcing ————————————¦————————>
Combining volumes to achieve discounts ——¦————————>
Area/global agreements ——————————¦————————>
Blanket orders ———————————————¦————————>
Export credit financing ——————————¦————————>
Payment guarantee terms——————————¦————————>
Exchange rate planning ——————————¦————————>
Packaging/handling options ———————¦————————>
Transportation modes ——————————¦————————>
Consignment consolidation ——————¦————————>
Commonality/standardisation ——————¦————————>
Materials re-use ———————————————¦————————>
Others ——————————————————¦————————>

Note: The dashed vertical line represents the desired outcome (e.g. project on budget or on-schedule completion); the solid vertical line represents the *improved* outcome possible when the positive external forces *are* anticipated and managed.

The result was, again, win–win – below budget and earlier completion – and the early involvement of procurement has now been built into that company's project management procedures.

If the focus is 'only' on achieving certain results . . . 'link procurement's role to the corporate strategy'

Many employees are unaware of their company's corporate strategy – what the organisation wants to achieve over the next, say, four or five years. In the 'household consumables' company cited in the first section of this chapter, the key elements of strategy are to deliver profit, produce cash, increase shareholder value and drive growth for the future.

But what are they for your company? Find out and then highlight the ways in which the successful achievement of strategy depends on procurement's input. For example, an objective to increase market share requires the company to have access to a supply chain which has sufficient capacity to provide more volume. Again, it may be necessary for a medium-sized company, without huge R&D resources, to rely heavily on key suppliers for the new ideas, as well as the products purchased. What is the buyer doing to make that supplier *want* to share new ideas with you and not with another more preferred customer? Again, your company may wish to grow by acquisition but does not want to get heavily into debt by borrowing money to buy other companies. Procurement contributes directly to maximising 'cash in hand' by negotiating extended payment terms with suppliers and by maximising cash generation through the profitable disposal of assets no longer needed. Major asset disposal is the same as major asset purchase – the commercial risks can be huge, only the sign is changed!

Table 3.4 illustrates another company's objectives over a four-year period and shows how there are several ways in which procurement must contribute to their successful achievement.

If procurement is seen as a key contributor to strategy . . . the message is that it also facilitates 'a primary business process'

Leading-edge business practices are increasingly focussing on the large-scale management of 'process' as distinct from 'task'. *Task* is what is done to deliver results, but *process* describes the quality, or lack of it, of the way in which the task is performed. Truly best results are only achieved if high-performing processes are in place. This refers not just to mechanical operations but also to the interactions between the people in the corporate team. The procurement process is identified as one particular sequence of activities which naturally links many different functions in the business.

Working towards the best procurement process involves making changes which beneficially affect the way the whole company behaves internally and thinks about its business – all of which is imperative if a company is to take and sustain its competitive advantage. This is the reason why just a few companies (but more will follow)

Table 3.4 Corporate objectives . . . and how they depend on procurement process

	Outline objectives	Depend on . . .
FINANCIAL	return on assets	lowest total supply costs
		more contracting out/outsourcing
	stable equity base	dependable supply base
		continual improvement
		stakeholder satisfaction
	liquidity	cash flow and cash generation
EXPANSION	annual growth	supply capability: volume
		technology
		contract out for others to produce
		'we' are an 'attractive customer'
PEOPLE	development towards	global networking (via 'CLAN')
	multi-national company	procurement as 'culture catalyst'
ATTITUDES	responsibility and respect	corporate image in supply market
		clear-sighted corporate teamwork
		(healthy inter-functional attitudes)
		procurement team as model of a
		high-performing organisation

are now reaping a double benefit from releasing the full procurement process potential which for too long has remained locked up in the company. They are getting the best deals *now* and will go on being best because they are using the procurement process as the catalyst for introducing the changes which will make them even better in future.

■ Strategic procurement

So what defines a high-quality procurement process? Here are some characteristics:

■ enabled, competent buyers providing clear leadership for the procurement process
■ thorough understanding of the relevant supply markets and the suppliers within it in order to benefit in the best way from the opportunities provided
■ excellent cross-functional teamwork in terms of structured decision-making and behaviours compatible with the developed supply strategies
■ specific supply-focussed strategies designed initially to achieve cost containment and then drive for cost reduction and contribute to competitive advantage.
■ absolute top-management belief that high-quality supply-side management is essential to the success of the business

If these prerequisites are in place, then 'strategic procurement' becomes possible. Strategic procurement is defined here as:

ways of approaching and interacting with the supply market which take account not just of the present situation but also how it might look in the future. It reflects the belief that the buyer can and should influence the supply market rather than accept it the way it is, with the aim of producing responses which deliver substantial cost benefits and competitive advantage for the buyer's company.

And when strategic procurement is happening, there is evidence to prove it:

- Time is available to do it.
- Structured processes exist which lead to key decisions being made as a result of creative cross-functional teamwork.
- Decision-making techniques are in place which turn data into 'intelligence'.
- Target-setting is truly ambitious.
- The supply market is approached in a strategic way, with buyers' opening moves being selected according to need rather than the dictates of procedures.
- Co-ordinated action across the company is taken by 'local' teams who are totally committed to an overall strategy.
- Results delivered are of 'breakthrough' proportions, usually far exceeding what might have been expected based on previous experience.

For many companies the above describes Utopia, especially in terms of the availability of time, and to think that it can be achieved is almost laughable. The reality is different: actually the laugh is with a small but growing number of truly world-class businesses who do not broadcast their success but quietly get on with being much more successful in achieving their corporate strategy than most other companies. One of the secrets to their success is the absolute belief, at the top of the company, of the need for the highest quality procurement process to be effectively at work. And note that they talk of cross-functional processes, not departments, so they are not crusading to put buyers on a pedestal. The key is people, and getting them, to work productively and coherently together: as they say, 'In this company we are *all* buyers.'

Chapter four

Reviving commercial awareness

Why 'we are all buyers'

■ Entrepreneurial, adj.: mindful of business

Technical discussions with vendors in order to specify needs are logical factual discussions free of commercial sensitivity. True or false? Those who believe that this is 'true' usually see the procurement process as a linear sequence of independent activities (figure 4.1) where technical debate leads eventually to specification and requisition, followed separately by a commercial discussion. The truth is that *all* discussions with suppliers present a commercial exposure, whatever the subject on the agenda. The problem is further aggravated if our specialists regard themselves as expert in what the supplier should supply. These are the consequences of partitioning the company's business into discrete cells of activity. Entrepreneurial small company owners have none of these problems because they see the entire breadth of the enterprise in one picture – truly a 'mindful of business' both commercially and in terms of understanding how different activities dovetail together.

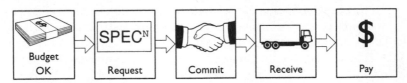

Figure 4.1 Functions in the procurement sequence

■ Specifying needs versus prescribing solutions

But let's return to the tendency of customers to see themselves as experts in what they want to buy. An IT company had identified its service contracts as holding high potential for cost reduction, the company's six-figure dollar catering contract being one of them. Discussions commenced with a catering supplier who was duly presented with a detailed functional specification which explained exactly what the supplier should do – and *when*, and *where* the vending machines should be put, and what sort of coffee should be used, etc. The buyer's challenge to the contractor was 'How can we reduce costs?' but, recognising that some collaboration might be appropriate, added 'and is there anything you think that we can do for you which will enable you to reduce costs?' The supplier's answer was unexpected: 'Yes, you can stop telling us how to do our job!'

The buyer took a little time to digest this since she worked for a company that had grown successful thinking that it always 'knew best'. Some new thinking and a new specification were needed. After some thought, this was formulated: 'OK, feed us!' At last, a specification which focussed on the intended goal and performance, not the 'how to'. The supplier responded with some probing questions. Do you have shift work here? From what social groupings do your employees come? What's the male/female ratio, and age ranges? Who would have thought that demographics affected the catering arrangements? But of course the supplier was revealing their specialist understanding of their business, which is why they were good at catering and not trying to make IT equipment. The results were far-reaching in terms of content and presentation of the total catering service, with the double benefit of delighted customers and significant cost reduction.

The moral of the story is that customers (whether represented by technical specialists, buyers, CEOs, etc.) should concentrate on clearly defining their needs rather than prescribing solutions.

Two lessons emerge. One is that internal users need to express their requirements in terms of the needs they wish to be satisfied rather than formulating instructions about what the supplier should do to satisfy them. In challenging users to do this, buyers and sellers must be able to present new ideas to users in a sensitive way so that change is not resisted. Many a new idea never comes to fruition, not because it is bad but because it is 'new' and seen as threatening by the user, who may secretly feel that they should have thought of it anyway. Resistance then goes unchecked if there is no accountability placed on the user for the cost-effectiveness of their specification, but the question of line-management authority and accountability is another story.

In a list of the top five ways of saving costs, 'changing specifications' will be found there, with more than 30 per cent cost savings possible. The key, though, is that buyers cannot do this by themselves, and internal collaboration is needed to achieve the big breakthroughs.

Just how big these breakthroughs can be leads to the second point. With many companies aiming to be 'best', quantum leap improvements are often called for. But don't waste time trying to calculate how far you can leap. Such calculations will be based on past experience, or what you have seen other companies doing. This puts a lid on goal-setting. Experience shows that company teams don't know just how good they can get until they start stretching for it. And if suppliers are invited to share that same vision and become excited to reach for it, then the sky is the limit.

What has been stressed so far is that > 30 per cent cost increments find their way into the supply chain by over-specifying, and by failing to engage the supplier's cost-reduction creativity. But the next threat is also an internal issue, i.e. the way a potential customer company behaves and what it says to suppliers in the course of technically evaluating their bid proposals.

■ Problems of 'a linear sequence' versus 'a shared process'

Solution 1: stepwise through the procurement process

So-called 'buying signals' can unwittingly be sent to sellers during early technical discussions. Some things will be volunteered by users. For example, a statement such as 'your product is best, no other suppliers can match it' sends dollar signs swimming in front of the salesperson's eyes. Supply costs will now be on the way up. Or, 'if you can tell me what your budget is then I'll do my best to squeeze down our costs to fit it' says the seller. The figure is obligingly given, and supply costs can now rise to that ceiling if the seller wishes. Users are generally highly able colleagues motivated to do their best for the company. The foregoing may sound critical of them, but the criticism should instead go either to buyers who have not thought to open users' eyes to the commercial sensitivities of early discussions, or to users who will not listen.

We mentioned earlier the problem of seeing the procurement process as a sequence of links in the course of setting up a supply chain. Figure 4.2 shows part of this chain. Technical activities lead to a requisition, and commercial activities lead to commitment to a legal contract between buyer and seller. It's worrying to see how many buyers see their activities as being confined to the 'commitment' box and having little need to contribute earlier. Figure 4.3 shows a new way of looking at these two stages, part of a parallel process with two activities woven together. Although early discussions, within the company and with suppliers, do rightly concentrate on technical matters, there is inevitably a commercial element in them as well. For as long as the buyer company's personnel are oblivious to this then the more they allow unnecessary costs to be added.

One way to translate figure 4.3 in a practical way is to take each step of the procurement process and show that all the way someone has a lead role and someone else is in support. But the lead changes hands depending on the situation. In fact it

Figure 4.2 Part of a supply chain

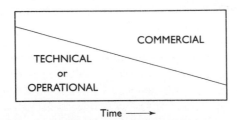

Figure 4.3 A new way of looking at the supply chain

Table 4.1 The procurement process

Main stages in the process	Lead	Support
Identify need	U	P/F
Develop technical and operations strategy	U	P
Develop acquisition strategy	P	U/F
Approve requisition	U	–
Identify suppliers capable and interested	P	U
Develop commercial side of the deal	P	U/F
Commit to legal contract	P	–
Monitor supplier performance – overall	P	U
– detail	U	P
Manage changes and claims	P	U
Confirm completion	U	P
Make payment	F	–
Manage stock	U	P
Authorise surplus disposal	U	–
Manage commercial aspects of surplus disposal	P	U

Note: U = internal user; P = procurement; F = finance

is this dynamic aspect of the activity which transforms otherwise 'boxed-in' functions into an interactive free-flowing process (table 4.1).

But awareness alone is only part of the story. Some non-technical skill is also needed in order successfully to avoid answering the seller's probing questions. Lies are not the answer, simply the politician's ability to sidestep the issue, and buyers have to train their user colleagues to be able to do this.

It goes further than this though in that potential customers have to be careful WHO they talk to and what about – and what signals can be sent to the supply market in the process.

Solution 2: an integrated mindset

Question to project manager during consultancy interview: 'How do you feel the procurement process can help you?'
Answer: 'Dick, whenever I think about supply-side issues I *am* part of the procurement process'

Let us now visit another company in the process of developing a multi-million dollar contract for a range of equipment items. Initial bids have been received from several suppliers. Evaluations show that no one supplier is offering the best bid all round. This means that supplier A's prices for equipment range 1 are best, supplier B's prices are best for range 2, etc. It looks as though the best plan will be to split the business accordingly.

However, as well as commercial evaluation, technical vetting also takes place and this involves further discussion with the suppliers. But what happens? Only range 1 items are discussed with supplier A, only range 2 with B, and only range 3 with C. Get the message? The suppliers certainly did and concluded that the customer company had already decided which suppliers were to get which parts of the total deal. No wonder then that it proved virtually impossible to achieve cost reductions in the subsequent negotiations, because the suppliers knew that they did not have to improve their offers to win the business. Only by a total rerun of the whole bidding/negotiation strategy were significant cost reductions eventually achieved – but having to 'go back and start again' is doing it the hard way and doesn't look professional to the supply market.

Many companies want to 'take cost out of the supply chain' and whilst much can be done here, a lot of this effort is unproductive in the sense that the customer company should never have behaved in such a way as to put those costs in in the first place. Cost avoidance has to be the prerequisite of genuine cost reduction and, if everyone in the company has integrated into their mindset that they are part of the procurement process, then much has been done to reduce commercial exposure. Selling the vision stepwise (chapter 3) may be the first step on that road, and it gets even better if strategic planning is the next (chapter 10).

Chapter five

How to eliminate waste and supply chain costs

■ Total cost of ownership versus the total cost of bad behaviour

All the good work achieved by optimising the Total Cost of Ownership can be undone by the Total Cost of Bad Behaviour.

Great emphasis is currently being placed in business on the need to reduce supply-side costs. Increasingly the focus is on Total Cost of Ownership, or Lifetime Costs. This concept gets over the preoccupation with price, and its attendant problem that the lowest priced offer can in fact turn out to be the most costly chosen once additional costs have been charged in during execution of the contract or the life of equipment. Further attention is then being given to reducing supply chain costs. Many of these efforts start at the point that a supplier or contractor has been selected to do the work. Undoubtedly much can be achieved when buyer and seller work together to understand and then reduce costs. Reducing inventory costs by better forecasting of demand and improved delivery accuracy is one example. But the uncomfortable fact is that this work may only be removing costs which should never be there in the first place: costs which have been allowed into the equation because of inefficiencies in the early stages of the procurement process. Chapter 2 illustrated this by giving examples of some 'bad' and 'good' scenarios. But being 'best' is the true objective and will only be achieved if a high-quality procurement process is in place which gives as much emphasis to behaviours as is given to procedures. 'Best Practice' cannot coexist with 'Bad Behaviour'.

So where should strategic procurement be focussed in order to realise 'break-through' cost reduction? Figure 5.1 points the way. The iceberg analogy is often used to distinguish between price (the visible part of the supplier's offer) and the submerged elements which contribute to total cost. It is better to call this the 'pr-iceberg' because it illustrates the danger and futility of attacking price alone. Quite apart from the negative 'price plateau' effects described elsewhere, attacking price is not the main problem. If you blow the top off the iceberg it simply bobs up for more. Better to get beneath the surface and attack cost. Figure 5.1 illustrates the three generic cost-reduction strategies into which most of the real breakthroughs can be classified.

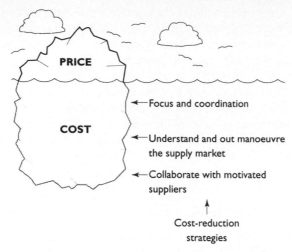

Figure 5.1 The priceberg (*Source*: Russill, 1994)

Three cost-reduction strategies

Control, focus and coordination of expenditures

This usually means the consolidation of several similar purchases which are currently being dealt with in a fragmented way by different parts of the company. The idea of bringing them together is to build a stronger position with the supplier and thus leverage volume discounts. The resulting cost savings are worth having and typically average 13 per cent. These figures also include the benefits of lowering the operating costs incurred in conducting the mechanics of requisitioning, order placement and payment.

Sometimes, coordination and focus enable the supplier to offer cost savings larger than might be expected simply from increasing volumes and moving down on the price–volume curve. One division in a company wished to purchase four motor-driven centrifugal pumps and already had offers from three suppliers to provide them. However, a search for similar requirements in other divisions revealed that 48 were required company-wide. Two suppliers offered 5–10 per cent price reductions in light of the larger volume. How generous! – but maybe that's all the buyer deserved to get if his negotiating style was to go straight from 4 to 48. But the third supplier came in at 50 per cent below their first offer. Two factors contributed to this. The new volume was sufficient for them to dedicate a whole production line to this customer's work, giving 12 months of continuity. Second was that they formed an alliance with the motor manufacturer who adopted a similar strategy. A nice example of dramatic savings (exceeding one million dollars) achieved through 'melting' underlying costs rather than chipping away at price.

In the main, however, coordination initiatives do not address *underlying* costs but aim at the tip of the priceberg. And the savings achieved may not actually be real reductions but simply a squeezing out of costs which should not have seeped in in the first place. This opens up a new aspect of 'coordination': the management of behaviours during the procurement process as distinct from gathering together miscellaneous deals.

Successful coordination of actions and behaviours demands awareness by all concerned of how their personal behaviour and decisions can adversely affect costs at each stage in the procurement process. Appendix checklist 6 at the end of this chapter gives examples of how costs and waste can accumulate at each stage in the procurement process. The overall result was illustrated in the 'bad' supply chain cost curve in chapter 2. The 'best' one comes later in this chapter.

Understanding and outmanoeuvring the supply market

Understanding the supply market implies working at macro and micro levels. The former especially needs the ability to recognise and deal successfully with market distortions as discussed previously. In addition, analytical tools such as Supply Positioning and Vulnerability Analysis (see chapter 11) often shed new light on how to solve old problems. The results can be stunning with cost savings in the 25–30 per cent range.

CASE FILE

'Overflow'

A consumer company was dependent on a single source for a raw material and, from their position of weakness, suffered poor quality service and rapid price hikes. 'Grin and bear it' seemed to be their lot. But they decided to ask questions. Two key points emerged. One: an alternative overseas source was found, albeit supplying at 25 per cent higher price. Two: the raw material was discovered to be a by-product from the local supplier's process. They had no other customers and the by-product would have to be destroyed if not sold. A new approach to the problem was now possible. Supplies were imported instead, the higher price not being an issue given the strategic objective. Now came calls from the local supplier: 'Where's your order?' 'We don't need any' was the response. The frequency and anxiety of the calls increased, as indeed did the level in the by-product storage tank. At overflow time, the local supplier was pleading for sales. 'OK', came the response, 'but on *our* terms, as regards price and service'. Price fell by 26 per cent with service transformed. And they have stayed that way, not least because options have been kept open by still obtaining occasional supplies from overseas. Easy in hindsight, but it took foresight to get there.

(A. T. Cooley, thanks Alan)

But understanding in micro detail requires knowledge of how the seller operates at the personal level. This is discussed more in chapter 15.

Collaborating with selected suppliers on cost-reduction projects

One of a number of goals may be in mind: faster service provision, lead time reduction, design developments, new specifications, inventory reduction. All such strategies require suppliers to be motivated to collaborate. How to motivate suppliers and the conditions needed for collaboration to be possible are discussed in chapter 15. Meanwhile, here's another real case which demonstrates the success which can be achieved through synergy, leading to a dramatic results improvement – not just once but in a sustained way. Field data show cost savings averaging around 15 per cent but the contribution to competitive advantage can eclipse them.

CASE FILE

'A Retail Legend'

A major company in Asia – we'll call it StarCo – has many large, high-tech retail outlets spanning the country. The business sector is intensely competitive. The challenge: to keep the customers interested, bringing their business to StarCo rather than taking it to StarCo's rivals.

One way to maintain competitive advantage is regularly to refurbish and upgrade each outlet. Of course, the competition works to a similar strategy. We'll call the typical cost indicator of each refurbishment project '100' (the actual cost being well into six-figure dollar sums). The usual time taken within the industry for each project is 180 days, and StarCo's actual performance is at the poor end of this average. Their usual procurement approach was to search out a contractor and award a refurbishment contract on a project-by-project basis. This meant that the contract company would do the best job it could in terms of meeting its customer's needs but, because there was no certainty of winning the next of StarCo's projects, there was little incentive to exceed the customer's expectations. For example, the contractor might introduce a new idea on the current project, only to run the risk of seeing the idea 'given away' to a new contractor hired for the next job.

Overall, StarCo had been satisfied with this traditional project strategy, although occasionally there had been some problems that created delays. Additional up-front costs resulted but, more seriously, each delay caused extra days of closure and a further loss in sales revenue. Increasing competitive pressure demanded a new response.

In collaboration with its internal customers, StarCo's purchasing team embarked on a new strategy – to stop the one-project-at-a-time approach and instead award a two-year deal to a chosen contractor. From the award date the contractor was treated as an ally, not an adversary. The other competitive suppliers were not forgotten, but were invited to compete for other miscellaneous contracts coming up, thereby maintaining their interest in StarCo and their motivation to supply in future. Psychology then came into the picture. The 'envisioning' process was used by the three-cornered team (internal user, buyer and contractor) to set improvement goals. Nothing less than 'becoming best' was acceptable, and criteria were set so that 'best' could be recognised when achieved.

Work began and, as project followed project, the team experimented, innovated and learned from experience. Further, the contractor contributed new technology as well as streamlining the work processes. But pause for a moment to ask what might at the outset have been considered a realistic schedule target. An improvement from 180 days down to, say, 125 would be 30 per cent better. Promising anything more would be 'pie in the sky'! And costs could well increase to pay for accelerated work schedules. As it happened, the team reached a point where projects were being completed for a cost of '73' compared with the previous '100'. And completion time? Sure the competitors had also improved down to 120 days. But by then StarCo was achieving 30 days regularly without loss of quality. A stunning example of a team achieving far more than could realistically be expected, not just in direct cost savings but also in terms of competitive advantage. Every time StarCo and a competitor commence a project at the same time, StarCo is back in business and earning revenues 90 days ahead of the competitor. The story also proves that 'breakthroughs cannot be forecast as an extrapolation of previous experience: "best" can only be discovered when we start stretching for it'. Anything less is merely honing what we already know we can do.

■ Getting it together: the 'best' cost curve

We've already looked at a 'bad' and 'good' supply chain cost curve, but what does 'best' look like? Figure 5.2 shows this and tells a different story right from the first step. Multi-functional teamwork ensures that realistic assessments of supplier capability and lead times are built into the statement of requirements, and procurement strategy development takes place alongside the user's technical thinking. Performance-oriented specifications are developed which then invite the supplier's expertise and creativity to decide how best to meet them, a welcome change from telling the suppliers how best to run their own business. There is close control of all contacts with the supplier, designed to stop the 'buying signals' which so damagingly reduce the buyer's leverage. Beyond this, 'conditioning' techniques can be used to lower the supplier's price expectation.

At the requisition point let's assume that the cost estimate is the best that can then be expected. The procurement team now takes the lead in using best-practice techniques to approach and seek offers from the supply market. The aim is to ensure that competitive market forces, if they exist or can be developed, drive the best deal towards the buyer. If competition is absent then a high level of negotiation skill allied to procurement marketing will 'win' the best deal available. Selection of the best offer will be based on an assessment of total lifetime costs, including the time-value of money and an objective assessment of 'soft money' factors such as the confidence and potential saving deriving from using a 'known' rather than an untried contractor. Commitment costs only 75–80 per cent of the 'good' base curve are feasible at this stage, but this may only be the start of the story. Real case histories show that it is seldom possible to predict in advance just how good the deal can become once buyer and seller, as a joint highly motivated team, start together to attack costs and 'waste'. The results, some call them 'breakthroughs', can blow the mind.

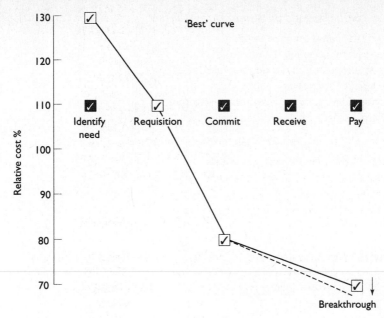

Figure 5.2 'What does best look like?'

■ The opportunity

There's no doubt that the winners in business in future will be those companies who look at their supply lines and expenditures afresh, not just as a source of significant cost-reduction potential, but also as a means of 'buying in' to the creativity and motivation of some of the best companies around who just happen to be their suppliers. Spending money is not a necessary evil as a result of doing business; 'investing' money in the right way with the right suppliers is the prerequisite for being in business in the first place. One challenge is to come up with the new ideas which, through effective buyer–seller processes, deliver the 'breakthrough' results needed to outpace the competition. But the greater challenge is to change hearts and minds within the company to the fact that supply-side management is a strategic activity needing the talents of the best performers in the business.

Making a real impact on profitability

Examples of 'Control, Focus and Coordination' include

Use buyer time and expertise strategically
Challenge the status quo
Change specifications and standardise
Stop 'careless talk' from experts and senior managers
Pick up 'careless talk'
Consolidate fragmented deals

Examples of 'Understand the Supply Market' include

Track and capitalise on price trends
Outmanoeuvre monopolies and cartels
Signal determination to develop alternative sources
Develop negotiating skills
Negotiate after bidding (. . . but *not* every time)
Understand seller's interest cycle

Examples of 'Collaborate with Selected Suppliers' include

Understand what you're really paying for
Understand supplier's business goals and cycle
Seek strategic synergy
Work together to remove wasted time and costs

■ Appendix: How wasteful costs get into supply chains

Origins of cost at each stage in the procurement process

Premise:

'Some of the costs we're trying to take out . . . should never have got in in the first place.'

Identify need

- ■ not a good business decision
- ■ unnecessary requirement
- ■ too short lead-time
- ■ wrong specification
- ■ over-specification
  - – quality
  - – time
  - – quantity
- ■ vendor choice limited or pre-fixed
- ■ unclear specification
  - – incomplete or ambiguous information
  - – specification concerns 'like to have' v. real 'need'
- ■ wrong people define need
- ■ buying signals sent to seller

Develop technical and operational strategy

- ■ not enough information about what suppliers have available to offer
- ■ wrong market knowledge
- ■ 'musts, wants, nice to haves' not differentiated

- long-term cost of ownership idea not supported (i.e. over-emphasis on short-term cost)
- contingency planning not included in total cost
- personal preferences go unchallenged
- an unique 'own-company generated' specification . . . not an industry standard
- supplier expertise not motivated
  - not exciting
  - limited contractual visibility
- no benefit from commonality and aggregation of requirements
  - other similar needs (within own, or other non-competitor company)
  - standardisation
- requirements too rigid (e.g. quantity or timing)
- duplicated, and uncoordinated, effort (e.g. technical and procurement people separately talking to supply market)
- alternatives not considered
- user resists alternatives
- stock safety levels specified too high or too low
- commercial exposure during early discussions:
  - buying signals
  - reveal budgets
  - reveal decision-making process and who has what authorities
- information brokering

Develop acquisition strategy

- make/buy/lease/swop, etc. not evaluated
- wrong contracting strategy (e.g. lump sum v. reimbursable)
- no systematic approach
  - key question unanswered
  - no strategy planning process with deployment of tools
  - rush job
- insufficient market intelligence
  - who is offering what
  - impact of similar demands (own and competitor) on the supply market
- supply opportunities not recognised
  - use of surplus
  - timing of entering market
  - distributor v. OEM and vice versa
- criticality under-estimated
- no longer-term strategy goal
- total cost assessment omits transaction costs (e.g. PO/INV matching)
- not creating competitive forces
  - alternative suppliers not developed
  - needs defined to favour preferred supplier

- reduced supply base
  - over-specification limits choice
  - demotivated when unsuccessful in past
- unambitious targets
- not seeing cartels
- monopoly seen as 'strong'
- lack of shareholder involvement
- no contingency plan for failure
- no bid-evaluation criteria set
- 'same' tactics used in approaching supply market for all acquisitions
- lack of new ideas
- advance/speculative purchasing
- need changes or disappears

Approve specification and requisition

- specification
  - is wrong
  - is beyond what is possible
  - is too changed v. original
  - is sub-optimal (over- or under-specified, or too rigid)
  - forces supplier preference
  - is too late
  - is misinterpreted
- specification does not define how quality will be measured
  - raw material or component quality
  - contractor service levels
  - equipment performance
- specification is not performance focussed (i.e. specifies the 'how' and not the end need)
- specification relies too much on supplier specification (hence costly when supplier changes)
- defective, or incomplete, approval

Approach suppliers and identify acceptable offers

- costly acquisition process
  - too many small transactions
  - overwork for 'low' order value
- controls on supplier not specified (e.g. basis/limits for sub-contracting)
- wrong information sent to supplier
- wrong market-approach tactics
  - misread supply market
  - procedural restriction

- no systematic approach
- poor bid–negotiate choice
■ too much information revealed about needs such that negotiation leverage is dissipated
■ lack of understanding of supplier prices and costs
■ better supplier not known about
■ insufficient supplier data (especially capability)
■ poor assessment of supplier capability and no visual verification
■ 'supplier drivers' not identified
  - business goals
  - pricing policy
  - at personal level
■ limited knowledge of supplier's enthusiasm
■ wrong assessment of value of business to supplier
■ technical evaluation of supplier offer reveals purchasing intentions
■ suppliers invited to bid when it is not seriously intended to buy from them

Develop commercial side of the deal

■ leaked buying signals
■ impact of liabilities/warranties not considered
■ mistakes/wrong procedure
■ lack of latest information on legal and government requirements
■ missed input from others (finance, legal, etc.)
■ lack of coordination (different functions do not work as team)
■ complacency since it is a repeat purchase (e.g. missed changes v. previous arrangements)
■ customer personnel allowed to be conditioned
  - by supplier
  - by themselves (we are weak)
■ lack of market intelligence
■ inside-out thinking
  - see it only from our view
  - don't challenge
  - misled/limited by own cost estimates
■ fail to create competition
■ unable to deal with monopoly
■ not assess value of terms and conditions to supplier
■ do not understand character/personal drivers of salesperson
■ do not have access to supplier's decision maker
  - have to give more concessions when we do
  - salesperson constrained with respect to concessions
■ pushing too hard on price (creates cost kick-back)
■ fail to achieve aims in negotiation

- rush negotiation
- wrong eventual choice of supplier
  - favour the 'known'
  - total costs under-estimated
  - present-value costs wrong
  - bow to politics (internal and external)

Commit to contract

- too long to issue: offer expired
- legally unsound
- local regulatory needs not recognised
- clauses overlooked or misunderstood
- verbal commitment without back-up: dispute potential
- letters of intent used too often
- region-wide contract may disadvantage local country operation
- terms and conditions not defined, or unclear
- lack of protective or performance clauses
- inappropriate terms and conditions
- supplier's terms and conditions
- unnecessarily long-term commitment agreed

Monitor supplier performance

- customer internal team does not agree on what is important to measure
- defective performance
  - not measured: no system or lack of time
  - wrong paperwork
- . . . and does not improve
  - wrong things measured
  - no feedback
  - no improvement framework
- excessive stock levels or waiting times
- no learning curve effect
- no dialogue to explore improvement possibilities
- not measuring critical suppliers
- measuring unimportant aspects
- supplier not made to feel morally obliged to honour commitments
- burdensome measurement system
- non-conformity ignored
- complacency: a familiar supplier is not monitored but 'left to get on with the job'
- negative impact if reciprocal trading goes sour
- supplier breaches contract
- fraud proliferates

- – poor controls
- – loopholes not foreseen
- ■ supplier goes bankrupt

Manage changes and claims

- ■ no contractual clause reserving right for buyer to make changes
- ■ high level of claims
  - – poor upstream work
  - – contractor policy to make claims
  - – user re-inserts original 'special' requirement
  - – change for change's sake
- ■ uncoordinated and verbal changes
- ■ unauthorised acceptance of claim
- ■ legal or cost impact of claim not assessed
- ■ compensation exceeds loss
- ■ lack of process/procedure for handling changes and claims
- ■ fear of alienating good supplier
  - – changes not introduced so as not to upset work plan
  - – penalty clause not exercised

Confirm completion

- ■ no clear picture of what 'completion' looks like
- ■ job not actually finished
- ■ no well-defined receiving system
- ■ unauthorised approval
- ■ lack of formal acceptance
- ■ lack of competent 'receiving' person
- ■ missing documentation
- ■ supplier delay
  - – actual due to inefficiency or problems
  - – supplier 'spins it out'
- ■ lack of feedback from user that completion has happened

Make payment

- ■ incorrect invoice
  - – administration error
  - – fraud
- ■ administrative work chasing documentation
- ■ funds not available to pay
  - – loss of credibility
  - – sued by supplier

- pay too much or too early
- no communication from receiver which triggers payment
- payment too little or delayed
- accounts-payable personnel do not understand special arrangements
  - e.g. later-than-normal payment
  - early-payment discount not obtained
- wrong payment medium used
  - telegraphic transfer v. banker's draft v. letter credit, etc.
- adverse currency shift
  - wrong currency
  - missed opportunity to hedge
- rebates not sought

So now that you know how costs get in . . .

you know what you have to do
to keep them out!

■ Reference

Russill, R. C. (1994), 'A template for total supply-chain cost reduction', *Electronic Components*, March, Asian Sources Media Group, Hong Kong.

Chapter six

Towards better procurement practice

■ Today's cost-cut problems . . . being compounded by solutions?

With supply-side management issues reappearing on the CEO's (or, see chapter 1, Chief Entrepreneurial Officer's) agenda it is not surprising to see business advisers springing up eager to be in on the action. The problem is that the advice often falls short of what it should be, and the action stumbles because the challenge of change is under-estimated. Many recommend that fewer people and dazzling cost savings are the prizes to be won, but too few have the know-how for making profound change. Thus the promised quantum leap turns out to be but an incremental stagger.

Too many assert the need only in terms of cutting costs.

> Too few are advocating a total, profound, up, down, across the company reawakening to the *fact* that it is the existence of a productive, committed, responsive supply market which *enables* the company to be in business in the first place.

The calculations are easy to do, the prize is worthwhile, and the punchline persuasive. One already profitable and successful company in the service business would need to save just 5 per cent on its total internal and external costs of $1,500 million to see the resulting $75 million savings push profit up by 25 per cent. But if cost savings are all that a company goes after, it's unlikely that they will be sustained in the longer term. Worse, it perpetuates the image of order-placing as an isolated functional activity, merely dealing with the supply market consequences of a business decision that someone else has made. It assumes that a cooperative supply market exists, and that all you have to do is decide what is wanted and then exert muscle power to get it.

The service company cited above earns total annual revenues of $1800 million. Subtracting the current pre-tax profit leaves the $1,500 million which is expended or, better, 'invested', in order to be in business. This investment (excluding capital items) is allocated between internal activities (people, infrastructure' costs, etc.) and in the acquisition of external resources. The internal portion is 37 per cent, the external 63 per cent. The management of external resources is therefore significant. In this context, supply-side management can be described as follows:

managing a large part of our company which we do not own, cannot see, and which is staffed by people who we don't employ.

Some challenge – and a whole lot more interesting than just placing orders. This management responsibility can be put as follows:

> The strategic purpose of the procurement process is to provide a high-value, low-cost supply base upon which the company can be successful in achieving its business objectives, and to secure that position by actively managing the company's exposure to the supply market and to competitor activity within it.

We are on the way to defining a role or mission statement. This clearly describes the intended purpose of the procurement process and the role of the team (if there is one) managing it.

■ Mission of the procurement process

In the fiercely task-focussed organisations of yesteryear (although many can still be found today) the task 'spoke for itself' and the task operatives who followed instructions did not need, and maybe were not encouraged, to question the purpose of what they were doing. Stating the reason why a job-position exists is very different from describing what the job-holder is expected to do. The latter often prevents good decision-making, let alone reaching creative decisions, whereas the former gives considerable flexibility to decide on right actions in the light of local realities. Today's leaner organisations, and the greater delegation of decision-making authority which needs to go with them, mean that people do need to be able to see how what they do links with the greater corporate purpose. Roberto Goizueta (Chief Executive, Coca-Cola) put it this way in a recent interview:

> We needed to establish a sense of direction so that people know where they're going. Then you can let them have a lot of freedom. But if they don't know where they're going, I mean, you do not want them to get there very fast. (*Fortune*, 11 December 1995)

Yet, many companies feel that a mission statement is superfluous. One reason advanced is that it is merely a piece of corporate window-dressing suggested by consultants and does not really mean anything. In a company only interested in management cosmetics, then, the mission *is* a waste of time. Here are some actual examples of statements which serve only to mystify and confuse:

1. To contribute to the maximum extent to the overall results of the company. Purchasing provides a high contribution to the company's overall profitability and has a key position within an integrated business management and overall quality performance.
2. Purchasing's role is to develop a total purchasing solution for which the criterion will be the maximum benefit which will accrue as a whole, taking full but fair advantage of our company's position as a major buyer.

But purpose and power combine effectively in a mission statement if it really does reflect top management's belief that certain tasks and processes should be given the right priorities in the business. And it is not only the statement itself which must be right, but other success factors have to exist. First the statement's content.

It's not just what you say . . .

Table 6.1 shows some 'historical' mission statements and the impact they are likely to have.

Why historical? Because they have been around for some time and each, in their own time, represented then-current perceptions of best practice and of the particular company's perception of procurement's role. The impact statements speak for themselves and reflect the inevitable fact that people's feelings about the importance of a function or process will be formed by what top management think of it and the 'licence to operate' which they give to the executive in charge. Saying 'nothing' usually reflects a management attitude of seeing the function as a 'burden' on the business. Describing things in terms of the right 'this' and the right 'that' positions purchasing as servant to some more important internal process. Statement 3 tells a much better story, but why is this still positioned as 'historical'? Here are two reasons:

1. Its adoption in a company often marks the time when management reawaken to the sheer size of total expenditures and their influence on profit.
2. In the best companies which keep moving forward, the 'profit-contribution perception' has been superseded by the realisation that there is a key role beyond 'just profit-contribution', often defined as contributing to the sustaining of competitive advantage. There is also the increasing attention being given to processes rather than tasks.

The notion of building up peoples' perceptions step-wise was discussed in chapter 3.

Table 6.1 Some 'historical' mission statements

Elements of the mission statement	Likely impact
1. Nothing stated	None . . . or at best a low status activity
2. Deliver right materials, right quality, right price, right place, right time	Efficient, reactive, limited to users' needs Internal orientation
3. Acquire goods and services required by users, delivered on time and of the required quality, manage the company's interface with the supply market in order to maximise company profit by obtaining supplies at lowest total evaluated cost	Effective as well as efficient Proactive/deterministic External + internal focus Seeking opportunities Profit contributor

. . . But also the way that you say it!

> A visitor to a company noticed a fine plaque on the wall of the headquarters' reception area. Closer inspection showed it to be the Corporate Mission Statement – relevant and well-chosen words. The mission statement came up later in conversation, but some of the managers weren't aware of it. 'You know, the plaque on the wall downstairs' said one. 'Oh, that', said another, 'but that doesn't apply to us'. 'Why not?', asked the visitor. Back came the answer: 'Because it was on the wall when we bought this company and took over the office. We left the plaque there because it looked good! Besides, to move it would mean re-decorating!'

Mission and vision statements are only worth their while if top management believe in them and if they are communicated far and wide in the organisation at large. Anything less is simply cosmetic window-dressing – part of the corporate decor. Neither is it sufficient for the Board merely to 'endorse' what others have articulated. Constant advocacy is what is required. If 'procurement' is clearly an issue on top management's agenda, then it will also be on line management's. And if it is on theirs, it is going to be on the internal user's. Ensuring sufficient and sustained priority for the procurement process is one of the prerequisites for strategic procurement to be possible.

■ Current best practice defined

Mission

A modern mission statement is shown below.

> The purpose of the procurement process is to create sustained competitive edge for the company by managing the acquisition of all the externally supplied resources, upon which business success depends both now and in the future.

For brevity the statement is condensed into just three lines, but even this may seem too much to some. The problem is that the shorter it is the less meaningful it becomes, but if it is long it loses impact. This dilemma is best solved by keeping a concise sentence as the 'flagship' statement, but then 'exploding it' line by line to illustrate precise ways in which achievement of the mission could be recognised in practice.

'Mission' really deals with 'today': what the procurement team and the process for which they provide leadership, was created to do. But then there is the question of 'vision': what we envisage the process will look like in future. This provides the motive force for change, and also a focal point in the future which will give a sense of direction for today's decision making. We'll deal with this later.

Policies and principles

A mission statement alone is not enough. Clear terms of reference must also be staked out to ensure the right standards and consistency of decision-making. But here is an important choice: will these fundamental values be expressed as procedures, or principles?

Companies which strap their purchasing professionals into rigid procedures are really saying that they do not trust the buyer but do have unquestioning faith in the supply market. Operating instructions which appear to provide tight control are in fact often wide open to manipulation by suppliers for whom it is easy to read a predictable game plan, and buyers are often forced to circumvent hostile procedures just to get the job done.

Business controls are indeed important, but will only be effective if they are seen as practical and relevant to the business exposure. So, high-class companies start by trusting their buyers and by being wary of the supply market in general. Typically they then increase buyer commitment authorities by quantum leaps, not fine adjustments to keep pace with inflation. Controls focus on key principles and policies which should guide the decision-making and behaviour of *all* those involved in the procurement process, not just the buyers (see table 6.2). The policy to do with 'Treatment

Table 6.2 Key policies and principles for best-practice procurement

1. Authority and separation of responsibility
2. Relationship between functional and business lines
3. Dealing with supplier visitors
4. Early involvement of procurement personnel
5. Joint procurement with other companies
6. Budget holders' authority to requisition
7. Company image in the supply market
8. Supplier relationships
9. International sourcing
10. Source dependencies
11. Purchasing from other group companies
12. Business ethics and corporate business practices
13. Confidentiality
14. Use of approved suppliers, and qualification
15. Enquiry types and formality
16. 'Best Value' basis for tactics and selection
17. 'Face Value' policy
18. Documentation
19. Approach tactics (bidding, negotiating, etc.)
20. Legality and commitment authority
21. Form of contract (incl. terms and conditions)
22. Contract award
23. Contract administration
24. Supplier performance management
25. Payment
26. Custody and disposal of assets
27. Delegation of commitment authority to users

of Supplier Visitors' is a case in point. Best-of-breed senior procurement executives then look for compliance with these core principles instead of demanding slavish adherence to procedural detail.

To limit one's personal authority is not to suggest that the buyer cannot be trusted with more, but simply matches decision-making *capacity* with proven decision-making *capability*. As buyers grow in experience, so more authority can be passed to them. But we find many companies denying buyers authorities which they are well able to use. The challenge here is to persuade management that 'delegating more authority' is not relinquishing control but rather replacing outmoded controls with modern alternatives consistent with the demands of business and the reality of a very complex and dynamic global supply environment.

■ Vision for the future

Mission statements are really about 'today' – that is, what the procurement process is there to do. However, what is needed or expected is often different from the 'way it is' right now. Changes are required to make the sentiments of the mission become reality. Since the mission statement describes the *role* that the procurement process plays alongside other key corporate processes, the statement as written at the beginning of the last section will apply in most organisations with perhaps only a word or two being changed to suit different situations (e.g. a government department v. a private company). But role is different from result and hence there will be specific task objectives which the procurement team is expected to achieve. Examples would be to achieve a particular cost saving, or to develop an alternative source in order to enhance supply reliability or to introduce competition. But for most companies there is an even more challenging goal to shoot for: a future state in which the procurement process is seen as one of the key processes at work in the business overall and as essential to the achievement of corporate strategy. This is now looking beyond specific task objectives to an all-embracing goal which inspires people to make change and gives a sense of direction to that change process. So, mission is essentially about managing today's *task* whilst vision is about *change* towards becoming better than other companies whom it is appropriate to beat. Whilst mission statements may be substantially the same regardless of company, visions tend to be more company specific. They depend on the current status quo in the company and where the company intends to be in the future. Let us look at two real-life examples. Vision 1 belongs in a company where

---

Vision 1

To ensure that external resources in all areas of expenditure are
managed in such a way as to ensure delivery of outstanding total
performance that will contribute effectively towards
all key corporate goals

---

procurement has been seen as an internal service activity concerned mainly with supplies of materials. Changes have started to move towards best practice. The elements of the vision statement bear closer examination in that they reflect best-practice thinking.

'External resources' suggests that suppliers have capabilities that can be drawn on rather than being mere sources of things we have decided to buy. Further, not using the word 'suppliers' escapes from the trap in which many users are caught – namely that suppliers supply production materials whilst other needs and services, often accounting for a significant portion of total expenditures, do not need to involve order-placers.

'In all areas of expenditures' establishes the point that all supply-side expenditures are to be influenced by the procurement process with the result that value-for-money and risks are optimised. But this does not mean that every transaction needs the 'full treatment' from hands-on procurement, because selective approaches will apply, ranging from user-actioned deals through to heavyweight strategic planning of critical acquisitions.

'Are managed' means that supply-side forces will not be left to look after themselves as would likely be the case where order-placers are seen as internally focused service providers. Instead, high-calibre teams empowered with best-practice approaches are influencing market behaviour so as to maximise advantage.

'Delivery of outstanding total performance' covers not just tangible aspects such as quality, delivery, prices, etc. of items currently being supplied, but the degree to which the supplier shares new ideas and selects the customer as their preferred partner in creating new breakthroughs. As one CEO puts it: 'If one of our suppliers develops a cost or quality innovation, would we be the first customer they call?'

'Outstanding' signifies the degree to which the 'breakthrough' represents a real quantum leap to new performance levels. In terms of cost reduction this might mean 30–40 per cent not 3 or 4 per cent.

'Contributing to key corporate goals' relates to the financial targets of the business and also to other important aspects of corporate strategy, for example, growing the sales volumes or breaking into new territories, both of which have direct supply-side implications. Indeed the emergence of a supply-side opportunity may drive a new sales strategy. If business is about making profit margin we can look to both ends of the business to provide opportunities to achieve it.

Vision 1 is right for the company concerned at this time. But since 'vision' is about change then one can expect the statements themselves to change as time goes on. This is right and proper and the trick is to keep the vision 'just out of reach' – not so near that no effort is needed to stretch for it, but neither so far away that it is seen as a Utopian irrelevance.

Vision 2 comes from a company which is further advanced in its journey to implant a firm belief about supply management's importance in top management's mind set. The CEO needs no convincing. It was he who asked the question above about supplier innovation, along with others such as: 'How do our suppliers assess our performance?'

Vision 2

To obtain long-term preferential treatment from the supply market which gives us sustained advantage over our competitors . . . and, in the process of achieving this, to create internal changes which lead to preeminent organisational effectiveness of the corporate team overall.

'Would we be considered their best customer?' Their vision statement reflects the importance of this question. They envisage a future state where they have not just a positive answer to the question (having perhaps implemented strategies to get there) but also tangible benefits derived from being top of the supplier's preferred customer list. And the reference to 'Organisational Effectiveness' reflects the enormity of the challenge to change people's perceptions about their buyer colleagues. Best practice can never be the bedfellow of bad attitude. It is the cross-functional nature of the procurement process which provides the opportunity to change attitudes en route to doing better deals.

Let us state it again:

The procurement process is a microcosm of the business overall and the evidence is that a significant improvement in the effectiveness of this process not only achieves direct cost reductions but more powerfully benefits the culture and performance of the business overall.

Certainly there are other processes which run right across the business but what is unfortunately different about the procurement process is the lowly status with which it has come to be regarded by business in general. Why that is so is another story, but its being a fact means that to improve attitudes towards it requires near superhuman efforts on the part of those advocating change, and massive re-thinking for the whole corporate team to 'buy in' to the fact that their roles and behaviours may need to change in future. It is the pain involved which makes the cure such a positive and lasting one.

■ Reference

Fortune, 11 December 1995, p. 52.

Chapter seven

Organising for a high-performing procurement process

This chapter is not just about how to organise the human team but also about how to organise the work they do. The two issues are connected. They say that 'form follows function'. The problem is that 'function' or role is often not clearly defined and so the daily tasks which demand attention drag organisational structure behind them. If the task gets bigger, we look for more people. If the task is not done well we strengthen weaknesses in the team or its structure. This evolutionary process has merits but, over time, can lead to an organisation structure that is unable to deal effectively with the challenges of the day. Advocates of business process reengineering will now say that this state of affairs requires there to be a 'revolution of processes and structure', but even this can fail if the goal of the team and the principles at the heart of the process are not clearly defined. In their absence, the sheer gravitational pull of task subdues effective process and the team is sucked into a high workload of low value-adding activity.

■ Organising time and priorities

In many order-placing departments it is like a gymnasium – buyers on exercise bikes working hard but not getting far. However, if this problem can be fixed then we have the opportunity to focus clearly on the goal we need the team to reach and then organise in such a way as to maximise their success. Buyers get off their bikes and into the racing car. But having buyers immersed in a high volume of low-value activity is not because that is the way they want it but because that is the way it works out, given the prevailing policies and the 'downstream' problems which fuel each day's fire fighting activity.

What can go wrong with policies?

One company spends £24.36 million per year, issuing 13,399 purchase orders in the process (an average order value of £1,818). Of these orders 9,865 (73.6 per cent of the total number) are valued at or less than £500. Under this limit, orders can be placed with any suitable supplier regardless of the price competitiveness of the supplier's offer: the 'face value' policy. Above this threshold, the company policy is that orders should be placed on a 'competitive basis'. This means that time has to be spent searching out the best deal, always assuming that more than one offer is available from which to choose. Let's examine what this means for those transactions in the range £501–£1,000. In all, 1,279 orders fall within this category. and the total spent is £860,176 – working out at £672 per deal made. Assume that an average 10 per cent price saving can be made by searching out the best deal each time. The reward for the effort is £67, but what has it cost to reap it? Two hours of buyer time may cost £50 plus, say, £25 to cover the system costs of issuing the order – and the saving disappears. And these are conservative figures. But what happens if the policy is changed (as it was in the real company) such that a competitive search is required only for deals above £1,000? The 1,279 orders are released from the competitive search process and they can now be awarded 'at face value', maybe without even looking for more than one offer. Significantly less time is needed to process each requisition, at most maybe only 25 per cent of what was taken previously: a saving of almost 2,000 hours per year, or one job.

Managers in many companies would now be pressed to eliminate this job position, but the smart ones (again as in the real case) reinvest that time in strategic purchasing. Assume for the moment that this means more time being devoted to orders on the £1,001–£50,000 range where a total of £13.47 million is spent, and that an incremental saving (i.e. over and above what may already be being delivered in the base case) of just 1 per cent is achieved. For one buyer's salary of £25k per year (doubling to £50k if other employment costs are added in), the 1 per cent saving of £135k represents a handsome return. Pressures on headcount being what they are, mathematical logic such as this seldom gains boardroom approval to go recruiting. Why this is so is another story. But the logic, simplistic as it is, can and does win the argument to change existing policies and practices in order dramatically to liberate the effectiveness and increased impact which is there to be made, bottled up, in an existing organisation.

The good news is that changing policies is only one of the possibilities available to improve organisational effectiveness. Options available to release more time include:

- introduction of 'face-value' policy, or an increase in its trigger value
- delegation of commitment authority to users
- call-off contracts
- procurement cards
- converting current 'items' contracts into service contracts (e.g. supplier replenished stocks)
- contracting out

The last option is especially relevant to Tactical Acquisition items as defined on the Supply Positioning matrix (chapter 11), but it is vital to remember that this analytical tool ensures that the 'costs saved versus effort invested' discussion does not ignore the presence and magnitude of supply exposures. These are the risks to the business involved in depending on external supply sources. So, the achievement of *cost savings* through strategic procurement is only one objective. First it is often imperative to develop strategies which deal with the *supply risks* and *vulnerabilities* of which order-placers may have remained blissfully ignorant whilst so thoroughly preoccupied with handling the paperwork and other downstream activity.

Why downstream problems?

Even if a sensible policy framework exists and other support systems are in place to streamline the tactical processes, time may still be diverted away from strategic issues because of the need to address 'downstream problems'. These occur downstream of the commitment point in the procurement process: i.e. after the contract has been made. The seeds for these problems have often been sown earlier on in the procurement process, and downstream work seldom adds value since it mainly focusses on resolving failures or damage limitation. Table 7.1 shows data obtained by surveying the time expenditure patterns of procurement personnel across locations in 14 countries within a multi-national company.

Table 7.1 Time expenditure pattern

(a) Contributing purchasing viewpoints to strategy discussions relating to manufacturing issues, and to the direction and goals of the company's business overall	8%
(b) Working with internal users to optimise requirements before requisition	8%
(c) Bringing together users and specialists from other functions to make decisions and plans at different stages in developing acquisition strategies	9%
(d) Out in the supply market and/or visiting suppliers to understand trends/capabilities	10%
(e) Working with users and suppliers to develop and approve new sources and products	13%
(f) Obtaining offers, closing deals and monitoring contract performance	18%
(g) Dealing with problems of poor supplier performance (incl. expediting)	8%
(h) Dealing with changes and claims	5%
(i) Dealing with invoice queries and other reconciliations	6%
(j) Producing internal reports, departmental administration, etc.	15%

Four types of work can be discerned in table 7.1:

- 'operational upstream work'   items (d)–(f)   41 per cent
- downstream work   items (g)–(i)   19 per cent
- administration   item (j)   15 per cent
- 'strategic' upstream activity   items (a)–(c)   25 per cent

The data, drawn from a company operating an already good and improving procurement activity, shows that a significant time is still being drawn in to downstream work which is essentially failure-related, i.e. dealing with problems which have arisen because of problems having their origins earlier in the procurement process, or in poor supplier performance. In another survey of nine sites within a company in one country, 33 per cent of time was allocated to downstream work as defined above. The critical point is that it seldom pays to attempt solving downstream problems by re-organising to handle them in a different way. Rather, fundamental changes in the areas of mission, policy, attitudes and perceptions are more likely to be the pressing priorities if a best-practice environment is to be created in which people can do their best in ensuring that the seeds of downstream problems are not sown in the first place. Organising the best way to play the team then becomes a relevant question.

■   Defining and locating procurement tasks

No one organisation structure is right for all time, but the best are those which, simultaneously, deliver today's task results and move forward in some way in terms of improving the supply position, or market knowledge, or the impact made by the procurement team within the business. For example the team could be structured:

- by 'supply' categories of items needed   to improve market knowledge
- by company functions/departments   to improve internal relationships
- by key suppliers   to optimise influence with them
- by tactical and strategic activity   to use skills available in the best way

The key is to organise the team in the way which gives the best chance of it achieving the desired objective. This is in marked contrast to organisations which have evolved over time ('we've always done it this way') or as a reaction to a problem ('reorganising shows that we're doing something to fix it').

If the company is small, with perhaps just one buyer, detailed knowledge usually resides in technical experts or users. This is good, the business needs them. But unfortunately this usually leads to a situation where they do the deals and look to the buyer merely to formalise them. Far better to ensure that, whilst their technical talents are indeed realised to the full, the commercial position is not compromised in the process. This requires the buyer to influence behaviours between the customer company overall and the supplier and to guide all interactions between them. The buyer, even if they are the only one, therefore has a process responsibility as well as being relied upon to deploy task expertise and authority in terms of establishing commercially and legally sound trading relationships. So even just one buyer has a bigger job to do than just setting up the deals.

In larger companies a further option arises: that of decentralised versus centralised activity. But it brings with it a dilemma: 'We can get a bigger discount by centralising our buying and combining volumes'; or alternatively, 'Our overhead costs are too high; we can reduce them by disbanding central procurement and let our individual oper-ating locations place orders themselves.' Which option has your vote? The chances are that you can be in a company and hear the first phrase one year, and five years later in the same company hear the second. Such is the ebb and flow of feeling about how best to organise the purchasing team. Let us look at the benefits of each approach.

Centralising procurement's muscle power

Figure 7.1 illustrates how procurement action and commitment authority may be organised in a sizeable company with more than one operating location. The central purchasing team is positioned at the heart of the company, headed by the Senior Procurement Executive (SPE). This team handles the company-wide strategic contracts and in addition will usually have an advice and guidance role whereby they promulgate policy and lead change processes. Out in the operating location(s) a significant amount of local supply-related activity may provide a full-time job for the buyer(s) located there. This is the 'decentralised procurement team' and, although located away from headquarters, it will usually report directly to the SPE. Some smaller operating locations may require the services of a local buyer, but not to the extent of their being full time. The 'local buyer' (one company calls this position the 'purchasing focal point') may therefore have other duties and report directly to the local operating boss, but importantly they are regarded as 'fully professional' whenever they are performing their procurement role. Finally, and in line with good practice, some commitment authority may be delegated to internal users, designated 'user buyers'.

The above hierarchy operates well for many companies but note that, apart from the user buyers, it preserves functional boundaries. Someone does the requisitioning, someone else does the commitment, someone yet again pays the bill. This can consume time 'passing the paper' (albeit electronically) between the functions but, more dangerously, perpetuates the idea that the steps in the procurement process are independent of each other, which they are *not* since commercial exposure exists throughout. In response to this, one company has successfully evolved the decentralised procurement team into being a cross-functional group which makes all the decisions necessary to operate the procurement process – a 'local procurement unit'.

So what are the benefits of the centralised approach? The obvious incentive is to be able to capture volume discounts through consolidation of what would otherwise be fragmented local deals. Focussing expenditure-reporting on a central point allows a

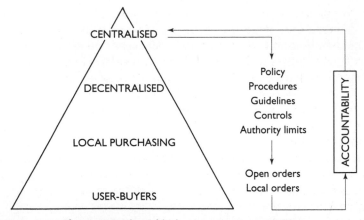

Figure 7.1 Hierarchical procurement organisation

total cost picture to be built up and shows just how much is being expended with certain suppliers. From the centre can come policy creation and guidelines, personnel development programmes, tiers of authority, delegation and control, and feedback mechanisms showing key expenditure-reporting, local content monitoring for government purposes, and the overall measurement of procurement performance.

If this sounds like an inflexible regimentation of activity then that can indeed be one of the consequential problems of the centralised approach. This well-organised army, bristling stiffly with buying power, may find itself marching in the wrong direction as local or global supply market upheavals present surprise and unwelcome changes.

The centralised approach may not be right for all the time, but at some stage in a company's evolution it is undoubtedly the right way to go. It is appropriate when procurement activity has been fragmented around the company, with many local arrangements duplicating each other. They all buy ostensibly the 'same' things from a myriad of suppliers, each offering marginal differences in specification. Up go inventory costs. By getting the act together, 'bigger deals' can earn better responses from chosen suppliers who now see the customer as having a more significant profile than before. Alternatively, split-sourcing may be better when the consolidated picture shows an over-dependency on one supplier for a strategic-critical requirement. Creation of company-wide 'call off' or umbrella contracts can also save time for buyers, releasing them from downstream activity in order to handle strategic issues. Bringing in major changes – a new computer system, or radical policy changes – is also best led from the centre, as is the need to reestablish control in the wake of a major control breakdown or abuse of delegated commitment authority. The theme, undeniably, is 'action at the centre'. The problems, undeniably, can be slow responses to local needs and isolation of local buyers from strategic activity, and, in the worst cases, competition between local and central teams to see who can 'win' the best deals. So, decentral-isation may be better after all . . .?

Keeping the buying local

In a totally decentralised situation all the action is out in the operating areas with no strings being pulled from the centre. This is in line with the modern drive towards creating autonomous business units or stand-alone businesses within the company group. Each local business will therefore have its own procurement team. How they choose to organise will depend on their local objectives as discussed earlier. One thing for certain is that there will be a faster response to the users' needs. And with procurement's role being more visible there may also be benefits in terms of being involved earlier when specifications are being decided. Maybe it is time for the buyer to break into those close liaisons that salespeople love to develop with designers and specifiers, liaisons which work so much in the supplier's favour, often without the 'prospect' ever suspecting that they are being targeted and conditioned. Perhaps there are *local* needs which are best met by local deals, and to bring in the heavy artillery of central purchasing is to overkill.

With full decentralisation, action is in the business. But, just supposing a supplier starts playing off one operating location against another? Or different buyers in different locations start taking *ad hoc* approaches which make our company look fragmented and unprofessional (undesirable, even) to our suppliers? And the head-count numbers of the once-slim business units begin to swell. Then the consultants come in and do the sums which prove that a central procurement team can do the job with less people overall. Maybe, after all it would be better to go back to the centralised approach!

And so the pendulum swings to and fro; time and energy are expended in the fruitless search for the 'best' procurement organisation. Is there a 'best'? Something which harnesses the best of both options and is not a compromise? There is, and it is a 'CLAN'.

■ 'CLAN': the network platform for process leadership
(Russill, 1990, 1991)

> One approach sometimes tried is to coordinate cross-business procurement on an *as-required* basis by giving a senior manager the task of making it happen. This is a valid attempt to achieve coordination by focussing on a process of interaction, as distinct from structuring a central team around the task. However the manager's own 'vertical' responsibilities to his or her own business get in the way of 'horizontal' across-the-business process management. Further, observes a director given this special responsibility, 'the process only works when I personally kick-start it'. In-between times, participants in the process are drawn down into looking at their local priorities, as opposed to seizing cross-business opportunities. The issue then is not 'how to organise tasks' but 'how to organise so that cross-business cooperation happens in a sustained way'.

Take a seminar of 40 people from different companies and ask in how many of them is procurement *totally* decentralised, meaning that there's nothing at all at the centre of the company. Answer? – usually only one. This suggests that in the rest there is some centralised activity, so now ask in how many cases all the procurement is done centrally, Answer? – again usually 'one'. So in how many companies is there a mix of centralised and decentralised activity? A forest of hands goes up. We seem to have accounted for all present. But not so, since a count-up shows that one person has not yet voted. So what exactly does this 'one person' do in this centre team if they are not engaged in hands-on procurement? Their primary interest is to make networking happen between the independent business units (experience shows that networking on this scale fails if it is not driven) and to provide CLAN leadership.

CLAN means Centre-Led Action Network and it is a real alternative to the centralised–decentralised dilemma rather than being just a compromise between the two. The network consists of fully empowered procurement teams in the strategic business units (SBUs), each reporting to its own business manager and board, and able to handle all the supply market issues necessary for that business to operate.

Role of network team
- Create local-buyer interactions
- Cause strategy development
- Set standards
- Sustain best practices
- Champion for procurement
- Provide process leadership

Networking across the businesses is achieved through the agency of a small centre, or 'network' team. The leader of this team is the senior procurement executive (SPE) of the company and sits at, or next to, main board level. Figure 7.2 shows how the team achieves coordination by providing a central focus for the procurement process . . . not just across functions, but across businesses as well.

Coordination through providing focus is fundamentally different from the conventional centralised model which achieves coordination through hands-on execution of a centralised task by having a permanent team set up to do it.

In the CLAN, co-ordinated action is achieved when it is needed by temporarily bringing together buyers from the relevant SBUs who then together devise and execute the acquisition strategy. One company calls such task forces 'focus teams'. A team will decide which of their number will effectively perform a 'lead buyer' role, and sometimes the SPE will guide this choice in the interests of the nominee's career development. In effect, any full-time member of an SBU procurement team is at the same time a member of a functional family (thereby adding new relevance to the CLAN acronym), and involvement in acquisition task-force meetings is one way of keeping the family in touch.

The data in table 7.1 shows that network teams do not need to be large, even if their span of influence is global. This in turn reflects the premise that the team's size has more to do with what it takes to 'make networking happen' than with the scale of activity. However, the numbers involved will change depending on what stage the

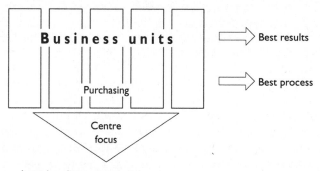

A total quality corporate team

Figure 7.2 The centre-led action network

Table 7.1 Network teams – how many people?

Oil Company, country-wide network	4
Global Telecommunications Company	4
Manufacturing Company, Europe	3
Petro-chemical, 14 Asian countries	4
Major Bank: country-wide network	3
Global FMCG company	1

CLAN has reached in its evolution. In the early days, considerable extra effort is required to kick-start and sustain the change process. Of the above companies the FMCG company's CLAN is some six years into its evolution whereas the others are only between one and three years old.

Initial activities and the size of the network team are heavily influenced by the need to facilitate the change process and to champion the cause. Table 7.2 shows one network team leader's view of what the job comprises and how the emphasis shifted as the procurement change programme progressed.

Table 7.2 Network team leader's role

Provide vision: overall and specifically tuned for each SBU

Advocacy: initially took 30–40 per cent of time, and still a key priority

Catalyst for change: initially considerable, now only 1–2 per cent of time

Ensuring collaboration across the businesses: now 'more the norm'

Offer procurement expertise and internal consultancy: now takes 10 per cent of time

Human resource coordinator

Audit and feedback

Ultimately accountable for effectiveness of corporate procurement process

Prerequisites for success

Centralised procurement means hands-on action at the centre, but in CLANs it is 'hands-off'. It is a brave company that is prepared to create a team which 'does nothing with it's hands', but it needs that demonstrable commitment to be made if there's to be any chance of success in creating what is apparently impossible but which many dream about, i.e. entrepreneurial processes effectively at work within a corporate structure. For if CLANs are to succeed, corporate attitudes and culture have to change up, down and across the business. The prerequisites for success are:

- at the top of the company: **belief** in the need, active support and a champion of change
- buyers **enabled** by best-practice policies and techniques
- effective **systems** infrastructure
- buyers **able** to perform
- receptive internal users **wanting** to collaborate

In most companies it is not like this today and without the above there are many blocking forces standing in the way. A programme of fundamental change is needed to overcome them, but one big step change is neither possible nor appropriate. Several phases are involved.

■ Route map for revolution

Pioneers setting out on the journey to bring about Procurement Renaissance (that is, to reestablish the procurement process at the heart of business) can learn from the experiences of others. Through observing them and working with them in practice the following priorities for the network team can be identified as they evolve:

1. **Advocacy** of the need.
2. Gaining **acceptance** in the SBUs.
3. **Action** in the SBUs (i.e. mini change programmes) which change attitudes and behaviours.
4. **Enabling**: building tools, techniques and systems to underpin, and grow, SBU organisational effectiveness.
5. **Achievement (1)**: Delivering strategic procurement results by facilitating processes within and across SBUs.
6. **Achievement (2)**: as 5 but involving the network team in a very selective 'hands-on role', e.g. key supplier account management.
7. **Continuity**: ensuring that the changes are lasting and that continual improvement is now routine rather than the subject of periodic special attention.

In practice some of these stages overlap (figure 7.3), not least because some early 'wins' and demonstrable cost savings are vital in order to secure ongoing support for the change process. As one CEO put it to the senior procurement executive: 'your licence to make change is renewed daily!' – and the honeymoon period following SPE appointment does not last long (*The McKinsey Quarterly*). But that is the reality for the

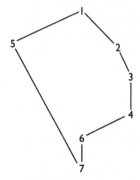

Figure 7.3 Side steps to step change

mature company as well as the entrepreneur in start-up mode: doing the business and growing the business are interdependent. CLANs provide that simultaneous capability.

■ Beyond task to process leadership – and beyond that to leading the way for change

Whilst the CLAN is a powerful way of making traditional matrix management happen in practice it has a fresh relevance in the business environment stretching to year 2000 and beyond.

Here are some reasons:

- The model provides room for growth: it can apply across departments within one business location, or be scaled up to embrace a global network.
- It allows the corporate body to 'breath out and in': additional SBUs can be added or subtracted without affecting the integrity of the network.
- It is flexible as regards local decisions about local organisational structures, recognising that some SBUs may be sizeable businesses in their own right. A mature SBU can have a highly decentralised organisation, whereas more centralised control may be appropriate in a newly created or recently acquired SBU.

Most significant of all, however, is that the creation of the CLAN network team really does challenge the senior management mindset at a time when headcount pressures drive in the direction of reducing numbers rather than creating new teams. Experience shows that CLANs can be born when senior management sees again the entrepreneur's vision of the importance of the procurement process to business. After years of expecting teams of people to justify their existence by doing tangible work (e.g. 'doing things with their hands', running central supply contracts), management is now prepared to set up a team doing something intangible like 'managing process', for that is the network team's ultimate job. In contrast to the task-oriented past, the discussion in the next chapter shows a very different organisational approach whereby results are achieved by focussing people's efforts through managed processes. Applying this concept via the procurement process provides an eminently practical and effective way of making the theory become reality.

■ References

R. C. Russill (1990), 'Unscrambling mixed signals on how to organise buying', *Electronic Components*, November, Asian Sources Media Group.

R. C. Russill (1991), 'Networking, or not working', *Purchasing and Supply Management*, January.

The McKinsey Quarterly (1991), 3, pp. 28, 29.

Chapter eight

Organising for process leadership

◾ The task tradition

Tradition has it that business teams organise themselves into boxes. Unfortunately we then behave as though we are shut tight in one. Why is it that we put lines around what we own? Maybe it is satisfying some deep-implanted tribal instinct. But at least it serves to define the edges of what we do do and what we do not. It clarifies issues like ownership and accountability. The trouble is that it also encourages turf battles: 'this is my territory so stay out of it. And maybe it'll add to my status if I take over yours'. Whilst these internal defend–attack games are consuming energy and creativity, the competitor is moving ahead. Typically, as we write, procurement organisations are *task* focussed. Whether they are centralised, decentralised or hybrids, these organisations essentially group people around the action, achieving work coordination by structuring who does what work. Figure 8.1, a 'task organisation', provides a general representation of the task-oriented approach.

Figure 8.1 is based on the idea, around for decades, that a big job needs breaking into many small ones which in turn are handed out to people charged with doing what they

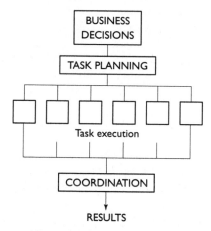

Figure 8.1 A task organisation

78

are told. But the hierarchical structure then prevents those at the top from seeing the reality at the front line, and those at the work-face cannot see the big picture. This does not deny that task structures have worked well so far in many companies. During periods of little change they allow activities to be optimised (or 'reengineered') and during crisis they provide a clear command structure. But they can go wrong.

Organisational structures, role statements, procedures and activity flow charts can and should represent the planks in the corporate stage upon which people can perform in an imaginative and productive way. But all too often they are used to mark out individual territories, each screened from the other, within which the players act out a preordained script without reference to other performers and without a license to interpret matters in a flexible way, the better to achieve the overall goal of the performance. Worse still, a task organisation laid out as a hierarchy can confuse as to what the corporate team's priorities really are. One company's organisation chart, laid out in the usual way as tiers of boxes, shows a line of 'key' headquarters functions sitting above the next row which deals with the actual operating or value-adding activities of the business. Unfortunately this unwittingly succeeds in suggesting that the 'operating' parts of the team are there to serve the headquarters staff who, as depicted in the chart, could be perceived literally as a burden on the backs of the 'workers'.

But let's be clear that task structures, even wrong structures, can work if competence and attitudes are right, and if there is clarity of purpose overall and individually. A company team can be successful despite having a wrong organisational structure in place. It is a workable situation but not an ideal one – not least because the rigidities in task allocations can slow down a team's ability to change fast to new challenges. Blurred purpose and organisational cramp are the real problems with task structures in tomorrow's world. These days, change comes so fast that an organisation may usefully see itself as continually being in crisis. The crisis will not be that the corporate ship is about to sink, but that we may be beaten by a faster-moving competitor or caught out by a new law or political situation. The positive part of this is that there is constantly the need to search for and implement new responses and, better, to set the pace for others to follow. The bad news would be if there was panic.

A good crisis may be that we haven't had a new idea today! . . .

. . . a real crisis would be that we didn't feel the need.

Towards 'preeminent organisational effectiveness'

Organisational effectiveness may be defined as the ability for an organisation 'constantly to be able to recreate itself'. This is a desirable characteristic but is it sufficiently results-oriented? Better to say that 'our organisation can do things that others cannot' – ultimately achieving levels of such high performance that it will deliver excellence whatever the outcome demanded of it. With the technology breakthroughs of the 1980s having introduced incredible flexibility into manufacturing processes, the challenge now is to create hitherto undreamed of flexibility of the human resources. But this does not mean changing structures to do the same job: it means flexible teamwork which proves to be totally effective even when the mission changes. Witness this real-life story:

> A notable real-life case cites one company's large production plant which set out to be the 'best' producer of its kind – and achieved it. World over-capacity then dictated that the plant was surplus. Total closure and dis-investment was necessary. The team said 'OK, if we can't be the best producer any more, we'll deliver the "best" closure possible' – and achieved it. A stunning result considering the operational, financial, environmental, political and, above all, human challenges involved.

That team thought in terms of 'flex-ability': an organisation still high-performed even though their *raison d'être* changed. This sounds fanciful to some companies perhaps. But others, the world's best (but not always best-known) are now achieving this capability, not despite people but because of people. With competing companies' systems and manufacturing capability achieving parity with each other, the competitive edge comes from people's talents, their personal energy and commitment and their feeling of connection with the corporate objective. Knowledge-based task specialists will have their place, but the drivers of business will be those people with the ability to reach across organisational divisions between different functions within the company, and between the company and external third parties upon whose support the enterprise is critically dependent for success.

Drucker (1990) helps by referring to the organisation as an orchestra. The big sound in most businesses now is 'we want to become the "best"'. The drumbeat is 'people and process'. We hear the organisation being referred to as 'an orchestra': the mission, the tune being played; the players all possessing talent, expertise and versatility – able to play more than one tune. The conductor, not *teaching* the players their own business and getting in the way of the music, but instead inspiring and focussing a process which stimulates each performer to give of their best – to the delight of the customer. Perhaps the analogy can go one step further to seeing the organisation as a jazz band. Wonderfully entrepreneurial in improvising to the very limits of personal ability, but never losing sight of, or connection with, the tune being played. If this sounds idealistic, then the good news is that we do know how to make fundamental changes to the way people think about the procurement process and their roles within it so that a real breakthrough in the total, company-wide organisational effectiveness becomes reality.

■ Procurement: the instrument of change

By virtue of its cross-functional nature, plus its focus on the commercial *raison d'être* of the business, we can see why the procurement process is now being regarded with new importance. Getting it right not only delivers a good commercial 'deal' and profit contribution, but more significantly introduces changes in cross-functional behaviour and orientation which are essential to creating an in-company culture consistent with 'being best'. In the leading companies it will be key business processes, not rigid organisations, which will be the means of focussing and coordinating the energies of people to deliver the very best results possible. The procurement manager's role will be that of 'process coach', not task-master. The emphasis will be on managing relationships, not individual transactions. Fine words . . . but, practically, how can it be made to work?

Old companies, new tunes: how procurement writes the score

Figure 8.2 is the traditional way of depicting the procurement sequence. Whilst this is good for understanding how different activities fit together it is nevertheless the 'task organisation' showing up in a more detailed guise.

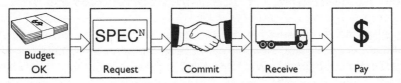

Figure 8.2 The procurement sequence

Dangerously, it perpetuates the idea that actions within each box are separated from their neighbours', and that 'step 2' does not commence until 'step 1' is finished. Whilst this may be a good way of representing a systematic approach with just one person being involved in the action, the model has limitations when the activity becomes multi-disciplined, real-time and multi-person. We need a higher-level representation of the procurement process, and specifically one which focusses on the Upstream Management of it, i.e. the stages, especially the strategy development phase, which come before the point of commitment at contract placement.

Upstream management comprises a sequence or cascade of activities, each having a goal which links back to the previous stage and ultimately back to the corporate goal overall. These activities are:

Supply planning: To ensure the existence of a supply market to which we have access and which enables us to succeed as a business both now and in future

Identify requirement: To define the true nature of our requirement, ensuring that internal and external interactions are properly managed in the process

Contract strategy: To define the right relationships and contractual arrangements via which suppliers can make a maximum contribution to our business

Supplier selection: To find the supplier(s) who can best achieve the objectives of the contract strategy

Finalise contract: To create a contract(s) which ensures that the supplier(s) completely meet all our expectations in a way which minimises the necessity for us to be drawn into unproductive downstream activity

(B. H. Court and R. C. Russill, Toronto, March 1994)

Indeed the first step, Supply Planning, takes its cue directly from the 'needs of the business' and sets out to ensure the existence of a supply market which meets the needs of the business both now and in future. A range of concepts, tools and analytical techniques are available to design strategy and plan action (see chapter 11, esp. figure 11.3).

The key is that the upstream management process involves cross-functional, maybe cross-business inputs – all we need is someone who has the responsibility to drive the process and to bring together all the parties and specialist viewpoints necessary for the decisions to be made. We are back to needing a conductor to provide this focus, and inversion of figure 11.3 illustrates the notion of the team players, under the conductor's orchestration, ready to perform.

But what will the new organisation, or 'orchestration', chart look like?

■ Process orchestration for 'preeminent effectiveness'

Before redrawing the organisation, the first aim must be to get away from the problems pictured by the usual structure of boxed-in tasks. In these, someone else has usually defined the task boundaries, having first decided (often without the input of the 'doers' with the know-how) how best the task should be performed. Even valiant attempts to depict flexibility by using the matrix-management approach cannot escape from the idea that each person 'occupies a box on the grid', indeed more than one company talks of 'task cells' and this does little to suggest anything other than people still working in the dark! Figure 8.3 provides a new look.

How is this different? Firstly, the whole organisation is shown with the goal as the foundation or 'founding reason', which is why the business exists in the first place.

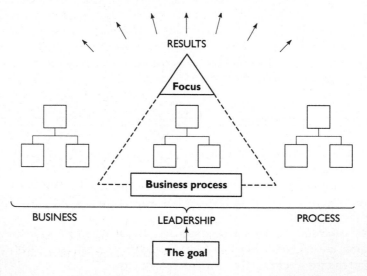

Figure 8.3 Results through focussed process

Conventional organisation charts put the boss at the top with no linkage shown to a goal. Somehow these pyramid structures suggest a bottleneck towards the top of the company and unfortunately this is a fair representation of the way it is in many cases: top managers as the checkers, nay-sayers, controllers and number-crunchers.

Our picture projects a different role for the CEO. In collaboration with two key types of colleagues who are responsible respectively for leading business divisions and key business processes, he or she interprets what the goal implies for future and current activity. Once this is done, the CEO's job is to inspire and facilitate the teams of company players to deliver the results needed. Through authority which has been delegated to them, each person is enabled to perform in a full and flexible way so long as their actions are congruent with the goal overall. The triangle represents people brought together to engage in a specific business process or sub-process. We are concerned here with upstream management of the procurement process, led by the strategic buyer who has that designated responsibility. The participants are engaged in specific task sessions (or 'performances') only for as long as it takes: it could be four days on a detailed cross-business multi-specialist strategy planning session, or maybe only 90 minutes on a supply positioning analysis or a final team talk before an important supplier negotiation.

This truly is an organisation which is constantly recreating itself under the guidance of people charged with deciding who should be involved and in what circumstances. Organisational redesign happens constantly rather than every three years with reshuffles between-times! The idea is to 'create space' in which people can come together in a flexible and appropriate way to make decisions and plans, rather than cramping them with the rigidity of predetermined tasks. But tasks do have to be performed and will only be done if people are given specific responsibilities so that they feel accountable for producing results, hence the inclusion of task boxes in the picture. However the overall intent is to portray the organisation as a homogeneous team (or, indeed, an organism) within which there are mobile processes of involvement between people responsible for specific tasks. But these tasks may not be 'fixed for all time, indeed they may be tasks which they undertook to perform at a previous 'process' session. So we now have the notion of 'processes' being the primary means of 'carving up the action' rather than doing so by pre-setting tasks which, once set, may not be precisely what's wanted given the fast-changing business circumstances in which most companies operate today.

> We plan sweeping changes to enable us to achieve the pre-eminent organisational effectiveness that is so crucial to our future. We must develop an organisational structure that reinforces shared accountability through multiple reporting relationships. The fact is that all employees have multidimensional roles in the implementation of our strategy. We aren't simply experts in one functional area . . . we also have key roles to play in the business decisions. To create the 'new company' we must embrace each of our own roles in achieving the goal.
>
> (Top *Fortune*-500 company, near to the top not just from size but also by achievement)

Organising around processes creates an environment conducive to highest-possible organisational effectiveness but in turn creates a key need for highly skilled process leadership, and a pattern to work to. And the 'pattern' consists not only of a structured application of upstream management tools and techniques, but also a systematic approach in terms of process discipline. The need for this becomes apparent when we examine the evolution of cross-functional teams.

■ Evolution of cross-functional teams

There are four discernible stages in the life-cycle of the 'cross-functional team' in its evolution towards high-performing teamwork being the norm rather than the exception.

Stage 1: 'dawn of the concept' This is where there is realisation of the value of the cross-functional approach but the type and content of these meetings is essentially the same as before, except that people from other functions are present. The latter may well think that they are doing the 'meeting host' a favour by attending in the first place!

Stage 2: 'functions at a cross-roads' These meetings have a clear 'task focus'. Participants will have been chosen in a purposeful way, drawn from their normal tasks because of the business or specialist perspective they are invited to bring to the discussion. Strategic planning tools and techniques (e.g. Supply Positioning) will be introduced and used within the overall Upstream Management structure. However, the meeting may reach 'analysis paralysis' and find it difficult to move forward.

Stage 3: 'progress through process' These teams exhibit the best of stage 2 but they now have a 'process focus'. The task structure is overlaid with a process discipline. This enhances the quality of the work done and the team activity keeps moving forward such that more progress is made than in stage 2 and the goals set are more ambitious. An essential feature of such meetings will be the presence of process leadership or 'facilitation'. However, these intensive 'away from the work' sessions will still be viewed as the exception rather than the rule. One problem is that participants will be 'psyched up' but will return to their everyday tasks wondering how they are going to find the time to put plans into action.

Stage 4: 'the beginning . . . and the future' The best of stage 3 is evident, but now as the 'norm', not just on special occasions. To reach this state, the operating environment will have changed such that people's value-adding capability is maximised through being freed up from daily routines, and a culture shift has happened in that cross-business multi-specialist teamwork is the normal way of working, with people detaching themselves only when they need to take actions to deliver the results for which they are responsible. Words like 'task' and 'cross-functional teams' may well no longer be present in the vocabulary since they are remnants from the task-oriented past. Indeed the atmosphere is like it was still further back in history, when the results-focussed entrepreneurial founders of the business were successfully growing it from its small beginnings. The trouble is that for many companies, 'growing up' also meant the onset of functional isolation. This is why many companies today hope to recreate in future what they were like in the past!

New frontiers for the 'boundary-less' company . . . and how to avoid old traps

The notion of the boundary-less company is achieving increasing prominence. In it, barriers between traditional functions would no longer exist and every employee would understand and adhere to the company's strategic mission without distinction of title, function or task. One major company's annual report goes further in declaring that it would break down not just its internal walls but also those which separate the company from its key constituencies on the outside. This is excellent, but in a sense it is not new because it perfectly describes the organisational set-up of the one- or few-person entrepreneurial small company. This is exactly where many of today's biggest corporations once started. Appropriately then, many companies are dismantling their vertical task structures and creating flatter, empowered, networked, process-oriented organisations.

But, unfortunately, many companies see the driving force for their change as merely short term: to cut operating costs and to rearrange tasks and authorities so that the fewer people remaining can cope with the more work left. This may be the only game in town if the company concerned is truly on the edge of survival. But the others who do have the time to consider organic change should try harder not to confuse what sounds good, i.e. transforming the business, with what turns out to be bad, i.e. torturing it to produce results. Some companies have now reengineered themselves to such an extent that one wonders if they have any residual ability to cope with more than today's task. Do they still possess the ability and the will to envision and plan longer term, to invest in relationships (internal and external) necessary for the future, to innovate, to respond to crisis? Lightening the corporate limousine is fine but it is not going to get far if the wheels have been reengineered off it.

Over-zealous removal of vertical boundaries therefore creates its own problems:

■ *Exclusive focus on process* One company declared that, now they had established cross-company business teams, they no longer needed functional missions and criteria for excellence. There also seemed to be little attention paid to harmonising the independent efforts of the horizontal business processes. Observation? Being in a process conduit keeps one just as much in the dark as being locked in a task cell.

■ *New rigidities and dependencies* Field evidence (*The Economist*) suggests that, for all their initial dynamism, network organisations can go stale. Because they seek to build close, long-term relationships with their customers, suppliers, sub-contractors and distributors, they rapidly become part of what is described as a 'stable network'. Further, networking can lead to over-dependency of suppliers on a single customer. A significant reduction in off take is then sufficient to bankrupt the source.

■ *Free-fall empowerment* Unleashing people from authority limits can cause a blood rush to the head. Empowered Managing Directors of subsidiary companies declare 'UDI' from their group parent. Empowered individuals begin to do their own thing which, although they are entitled to act, calls into question the business sense of it.

Many companies are beginning to see such signs. Just as these were predictable at the outset, equally predictable is the management reaction which will inevitably come soon when it is concluded that the new way does not work: reinstate control and authority at the centre and go back to issuing instructions.

The issue on which the success of removing boundaries and empowerment depends is 'control'. Empowerment is not a question of relinquishing control but about establishing appropriate controls for the new modus operandi. This echoes the notion of the Centrepreneur introduced in chapter 1. Old boundaries need replacing with new boundaries or, better, with new frontiers.

Some old control boundaries
■ Keeping people in the dark
■ Authority limits
■ Job descriptions
■ 'You're a task specialist'
■ Short-term plans
■ Procedures and instructions
■ Task accountability

Markers for new frontiers
■ Motivating business vision and goals
■ Authority
■ Business and process leadership roles
■ 'You're part of a business and its' processes'
■ Strategic plans
■ Founding values, policies and principles
■ Accountability for results and process

Procurement Renaissance introduces specific ways in which the new frontier markers can be described, and it is because they are specific and tangible that they are able to convert abstract notions into reality. This book describes some of them: for example the role of the CLAN network leader and eminently sensible, but fundamental, policies and principles which provide central points of reference around which there is the open space for decision-making and action (a marked contrast to having to operate within the stifling confines of procedural walls).

The old way was to define **what** decisions people were allowed to make . . .
the new is to define the **manner** in which decisions can be made, and **why**.

Thus the organisation develops its competence to deal successfully in constantly changing scenarios and get better than the competition, rather than to fall behind them honing old tasks to perfection.

■ References

Drucker, Peter F. (1990), *Managing for the Future*, Butterworth Heinemann.
The Economist, 10 October 1992.

Chapter nine

Towards best, then better, practice: the challenge of change

The pressure on companies to become lean, agile and effective is enormous. The only certainty ahead is 'uncertainty'. So, whilst the next millennium may bring us the ability to foretell the future, we have in the meantime to rely on 'our' company being better than the others at predicting what might lie ahead, and being better at taking advantage of change and new opportunities. The key is people, not technology. New technology which 'our' people have invented may give us temporary competitive edge, but only until someone else copies it. Then we have to think again. Maybe a smarter idea is to let someone else sweat out the new technology breakthrough, and then have our people think of innovative ways of using it.

It is especially relevant therefore that a number of current management initiatives are people-related, and usefully coming together in a clear way for the first time. It is especially tragic that many companies are missing both points and are instead destroying rather than energising the spirit of the company.

■ Why initiatives are 'coming together'

'Total Quality' reminds companies why they're in business and has set new standards for performance targets. Empowerment is 'in' at the personal level, and it needs to be if it is going to be possible for leaner organisations to produce useful outputs from their labours. The call for streamlining and synergy across functions and across businesses is answered by 'Business Process Reengineering' (BPR), itself derived from the well-understood but not often practised philosophy that 'best' task results can only be achieved by effective management of process. And 'best' is what the already good companies are envisioning they will become in future. Only by reaching out for that goal will they retain competitive advantage. 'Best-Practice Benchmarking' is relied on to check how well they make progress. But even at this exalted level of performance it is possible to discern two types of company. First, the ones who seek merely to find out someone else's best practice in order to impose it on their own workforce seem to be saying that 'we don't want to lose'. In contrast, the companies who constantly strive to get better are the ones who truly exhibit the 'we want to win' mentality. Sure, they look and listen to what's going on outside their company, but it is their own people who are regarded as the primary drivers of innovation and change.

■ Why change can be tragic

The problem is that too many companies look for the quick fix, the 'bolt-on' solution. When it becomes apparent that the current 'cure' is not working then it is rejected and a new remedy tried. This gives a useful appearance of activity. But much of it is unproductive in that it only fixes symptoms, not causes. More dangerous, it creates sceptics out of the once-motivated employees who now delay taking any 'improvement' actions because the current initiative will soon be discredited and replaced with another. Business Process Reengineering is in danger of going this way. It was only in 1993 that Hammer and Champy advocated BPR as 'the fundamental rethinking and radical redesign of business processes to achieve dramatic improvements in critical, contemporary measures of performance, such as cost, quality, service and speed'. And yet a recent business journal observed that 'reengineering has made us angry'. Look around and the evidence is everywhere. Layers of people have been scythed away from companies, taking their stress and disillusionment out of sight into the privacy of their families. What stays visible is the few left at work, now over-loaded to the extent that still-talented but less-motivated people are reduced to the role of 'process operatives' rather than being the original thinkers and implementers of solutions to company problems.

A look at one multi-national company's procurement process model (all 147 pages of it) reveals the extent to which companies have apparently become people-hostile. In the entire document describing the model, the words 'person' or 'people' appeared but twice, and only then in terms of their position on a process spread-sheet. But 'activity party' was preferred to the extent that it appeared 18 times on the first page alone – it seemed pointless to count further. In many other companies the reengineering initiative is solely aimed at reducing manpower numbers and has little interest in making dramatic improvement in organisational effectiveness. No wonder that the energy which people bring to work is being dissipated as anger rather than fuelling the power-house of creative potential which is present in any human team.

Sadly, the problem is not with the concepts, but with the cavalier and unthinking way in which many companies try to apply them. The use of new words and new flow-charts to describe what we do today in order merely to find efficiency savings will never achieve the quantum leap towards where we envision we need to be in future. A real danger is that whilst we may define a good 'should' process for today it may not be relevant for the future. It seems also that, in the rush to break out of vertical task or functional silos, we are herding people down horizontal process conduits.

■ The real challenge: procurement Renaissance

Many business change programmes currently in play are rightly driven by cost-reduction incentives, but only see things in terms of optimising what is being done now. This amounts to tinkering with the mechanics of the business: thinking 'outside the box' is not on the agenda. Reducing costs does make today's 'box' smaller and more efficient, but corporate capability at best stays constrained, and at worst is damaged. Little is done to create new capabilities for the future in terms of revitalising organisational effectiveness to make planned change and to capture unexpected opportunities.

Turning to the supply side of the business therefore, many advisers and gurus can be seen recommending the need to cut costs, and indeed the prize is a big one. 'But if that's all you're going after, then it perpetuates the image of procurement as an isolated functional activity, dealing with the supply market consequences of a business decision someone else has made. It assumes that a supply market exists and all you have to do is exert muscle power to get what you want.' Evidence of this can be found in those companies who are staking their cost-reduction success on the use of muscle power, or Tactical Leverage.

Tactical Leverage means optimising current transactions to prise cost savings from bigger deals. Certainly some real costs can be eliminated through economies of scale and it is also expected that the supplier should be willing to yield some of their profit margin back to the buyer in recognition of the larger commitment the buyer has made. But the fact that cost savings derive from such sources means that there is a cap on the total savings which may be realised.

If this is what happens in the good companies, then the best go an important step further. They combine muscle power (Tactical Leverage) with brain power (i.e. Strategic Procurement). This has been defined above (chapter 3).

Strategic Procurement paves the way for two additional strategies which achieve significant cost reduction over and above Tactical Leverage. They are: 'Collaboration with Selected Suppliers'; and 'Understanding and Outmanoeuvring the Supply Market', and were discussed in more detail in chapter 5. All three strategies may be in play at the same time, but *not* on the same item being acquired from the supply market. The precise strategy chosen depends on the nature of the specific supply market and the criticality of the acquired item or service to the customer's business.

Strategic Procurement differs from Tactical Leverage in a number of ways but the key point is as follows:

> **Tactical Leverage** is what buyers do, frequently acting in isolation from other functions in the business, and often by means of coordinating their supply-side needs via corporate agreements.
>
> **Strategic Procurement** is what a company team does before, during and after the point of contract.
>
> **Leverage** is a functional thing driven by consolidating separate requisitions: strategic activity is a process which influences and links supply market behaviour directly to the current and future needs of the business overall.

A three-pronged strategic procurement approach is better than one-shot tactical leverage because it:

- looks beyond price and attacks the supply cost base
- looks beyond the transaction and into relationships, engaging, where appropriate, supplier expertise and innovation

- detects and outmanoeuvres exploitative supply market behaviour
- links supply market responses directly to the requirements of the business
- develops supply markets to become what the business needs them to be

The problem is that conditions in most companies are not yet suitable for Strategic Procurement to work. A major change is needed to create the right conditions, i.e. 'Procurement Renaissance'. So, whilst the popular, and easier, option is leveraging cost reductions, 'Procurement Renaissance requires a total , profound, up, down, across the company reawakening to the fact that it is the existence of a productive, committed, responsive supply market which enables the company to be in business in the first place'.

So what is needed?

Focussing on the purpose of the business and clarifying the principles around which processes need to take place are prerequisites for success. Believing that the answers about what to do will automatically reveal themselves once we have flow-charted today's process as a network of tasks is to travel more in hope than in certainty of arriving at best practice. Process Reengineering and flow-chart 'prescriptions' may deal with today's problem but do little for tomorrow. Indeed they can damage tomorrow's performance by building in and perpetuating today's less-than-good practice. What we need are higher level process orchestrations which keep a sharp focus on the ultimate destination of the business and clearly show milestones of decision-making, at which points different people (e.g. technical specialists, budget holders, those with delegated authorities, etc.) gather to take action; their efforts focussed by the process conductor.

The key is to avoid telling talented people how to do the job for which their experience and trained-in skills have made them competent, whilst still setting out sufficiently clear ground-rules so that they know what the game is and what their part is in it. Creating the conditions for focussed high performance is more likely to stimulate a talented player to make fine music than telling them how to blow their own trumpet. The problem with defining universal best practice so that others in the company will follow it is that each and every foreseeable situation has to be anticipated and mapped out beforehand. Copious and unusable instructions are the result. It is better to define conditions in such a way that the performers have freedom to interpret situations and to apply their talents in an appropriate manner.

How to rise above the barriers to change

Barriers stand in the way: figure 9.1 shows the key areas where change is needed and where resistance may be expected. The point is that a holistic change is required: removing all barriers but one still leaves a bar to progress. Holistic, organic change settles for nothing less than the following goals:

(a) a platform or environment which motivates high performance

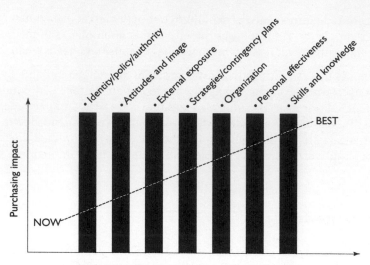

Figure 9.1 Barriers to beat to become 'best'

(b) a mix of talents with individuals bringing different yet complementary skills to the table
(c) instruments to deploy
(d) a game plan or 'score' to work with
(e) people who are enabled by the operating frame within which they work and not constrained by rigid procedures or over-control

Thus the enabling environment is created and what follows in Part II provides much more in the way of tools and templates to help the procurement task. But chiefly, successful change requires a license to take action which must be won by advocating the case for change at board level, using the beliefs and arguments set out in chapters 2 and 3, and then designating a change agent with the full-time responsibility for catalysing the change process. The 'critical mass' for change is well on the way to being assembled, but all ingredients must be present. Figure 9.2 illustrates what is needed, but also reveals a potential problem.

Assembling the critical mass for change

Starting top left and going anticlockwise in figure 9.2 shows 'authority'. This is the license to make change which is won by getting the Board to agree a mission statement for the procurement process together with the support to make change to bring it into practice. Then there is 'process and resources'. This represents the organisational and process operating framework, plus competent people to drive these processes, i.e. the vehicle whereby procurement plans can be moved into action. 'Strategy' defines the specific routes it is intended to take to set up deals today and to achieve relevant

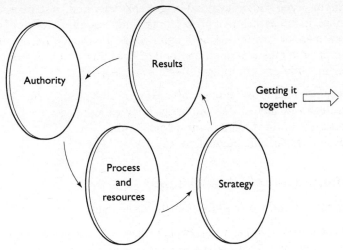

Figure 9.2 Assembling the critical mass

goals 'tomorrow' for all the external resources required by the business. And results, if they are achieved and if they meet or exceed expectations, speak for themselves. Figure 9.3 shows the potential problem.

The full benefit of change will not be realised if the critical mass is not assembled. Figure 9.3 shows one company's attempt at making a short cut. They felt that it was not necessary to get full buy-in from the Board to doing things differently, especially if that meant wasting time on theoretical mission statements. Accordingly, procurement's new initiatives were seen by the company as a whole as an isolated activity affecting

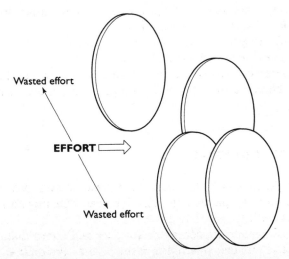

Figure 9.3 Incomplete change . . . no breakthrough

that department alone. Some cost savings were delivered, but these failed to get anywhere near to breakthrough proportions and certainly nothing was done to revitalise commercial awareness and behaviours in the corporate team overall. Likewise, other problems emerge if any one of the other components of the critical mass are absent. Only one component needs to be missing:

- No licence – means low impact and no supported strategy for change
- No strategy – means wasted resources 'busy going nowhere'
- No processes and resources – means no results
- No results – means losing the licence

Checklist for procurement renaissance

Complete, profound and worthwhile change will lead to:

1. A company environment in which proper priority is given to the management of the supply side, and the activity is one in which virtually all players in the company team understand that they have a part to play.
   This requires
   – belief in the need (see chapter 2)
   – belief in the mission (see chapter 6)
   – advocacy (see chapter 3)
   – enabling policies and principles (see chapter 6)
   – everyone 'being a buyer' (see chapter 4)
2. Effective collaboration and teamwork
   – across functions (see chapter 8)
   – networked across businesses via CLAN (see chapter 7)
   – with selected motivated suppliers (see chapter 15)
3. Analytical tools and decision-making techniques (see chapter 11)
4. An organised approach to decision-making
   – the Upstream Management steps (see chapter 8)
   – the strategy template (see chapter 10)
5. A Senior Procurement Executive (SPE) who carries the authority to provide leadership for the procurement process at macro (and, if necessary, micro) levels (see chapter 7)

■ Good-buy to best practice

Procurement Renaissance delivers more than best-practice procurement process because the nature of the painful changes involved can transform organisational effectiveness. This is illustrated in figure 9.4

Breakthrough task results are achieved. But over and above that, a new organisational competence is created, referred to elsewhere as Pre-eminent Organisational Effectiveness. This means being able to do things that other organisations cannot.

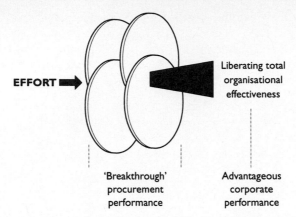

EFFORT

Liberating total
organisational
effectiveness

'Breakthrough'
procurement
performance

Advantageous
corporate
performance

Figure 9.4 Our organisation can do things . . . that others cannot

Company teams having this ability are versatile in the face of change and are able to work to new missions as effectively as they did to the old, producing new results long before their competitors who have been caught having to take time out to reorganise and refocus their people. Thus it is that the company which has successfully revived its entrepreneurial commercial processes and mindsets, has also created for itself the capacity to reach beyond today's excellent performance to set new standards for others to follow tomorrow. Indeed: 'Good-Buy to Best Practice'.

Part II

Chapter ten

Good strategies are 'nice' strategies!

We live in a demanding business age. The pressures of high costs and low margins demand cautious yet urgent decision-making. But the urge 'to be the best in the business' requires companies to make a quantum leap forward, maybe into the unknown. The real challenge is to achieve the best of both worlds: keeping a prudent eye on the business *and* having an imagination and courage which raise people's sights from being merely 'good' today to becoming 'the best' in tomorrow's world.

This sets the tone for Strategic Procurement, defined here as:

> ways of approaching and interacting with the supply market which take account not just of the present situation but also of how it might look in the future. It reflects the belief that the buyer can and should influence the supply market rather than accept it the way it is, with the aim of producing responses which deliver substantial cost benefits and competitive advantage for the buyer's company.

The challenge is not just to make a good deal today, but at the same time to create a situation which improves things for the future. The idea of strategy is to provide a direction in which to go, along with a clear goal statement which defines where we want to get to. Today's deals are steps along that road towards the desired future state.

One real company's situation provides an example of an ambitious goal statement. About 17 per cent of its total spend in the supply market goes on one key raw material 'X'. Without it, production stops. There is no bigger single buyer in the world for it, yet the supply market treats the customer in an exploitative way. Prices have just increased by more than 50 per cent, obliterating the customer's profit margin in the process. Definitely, 'X' is a candidate for strategic procurement. The planning meeting took four days, with nine people throughout, each providing various business, technical, operational and financial inputs. The goal statement appeared about

---

The future goal – raw material 'X'

A responsive yet secure supply of 'X' acquired from a supply market which
we influence to produce a significantly advantageous price which enables
our business consistently to sustain a predictable non-volatile gross margin
of 'm' and to achieve its other financial targets'

---

half-way through, riding on the back of 18 mandays of analysis. It could have been written after only 20 minutes. The difference is that the 20-minute statement would stay a dream, whereas 18 mandays know how to make it reality.

■ Template for a strategic plan

Many attempts at setting out the strategic planning approach get complicated by trying to cope with everything at once: the contents of the plan, the tools and techniques used in developing it, and the process whereby the result is produced. Let us take them separately:

Contents: the position paper

Think in terms of the finished document. If the strategy is important then documentation needs to exist, not least to provide the vehicle by which top management approval is obtained – just like getting Board agreement to, say, a new capital investment. If time is short, the bare bones would comprise just four elements.

1. What the acquisition is about
2. Why it is important to the business
3. Strategic positioning statements:
   – the way it is *now*
   – the *future* state we envision
4. Elements of the strategic plan

. . . and all on one side of paper.

And always it is vital to phrase things in terms of the overall needs of the business: that way it grabs management attention, whereas a statement like 'we need a contract to buy "t" tons per year of material "X"', whilst factually correct, is too focussed on the day-to-day mechanisms of business to be seen as strategically significant. Higher level interest attends statements like 'we need to protect our profit margin by establishing secure and price-stable source(s) for "t" tons of raw material "X"'.

A more detailed strategy document would present additional information along the following lines:

Strategic plan for the acquisition of 'X'

1. **The item (materials, services, knowledge) which is the subject of this strategy**
2. Data about the *current* situation in terms of needs (e.g. end-use, including the needs of the business as well as needs of the process, volumes, etc.)
3. Data about the *future* situation in terms of needs (similar to above, but also clearly linked to the corporate strategy statement for the future)

4. Current source(s) and contract arrangements
5. **Why the acquisition is important to our business**
6. Analysis:
    – strategic positioning of the acquisition
    – current prices/costs plus past and future trends
    – supply market situation (current and trends)
    – suppliers' current and future positions
    – buyer's strength in the supply market
    – our competitor activity (changes and trends)
    – internal activity (changes and trends within our company)
    – external activity (e.g. political, fiscal, legal, technology, environmental, etc.)
7. **Strategic positioning statements:**
    – current situation
    – future state: the goal envisaged (using the 'NICE' formula, see below)
8. Definition of the key driving and blocking forces, observed between the 'now' and 'future' states, which will be addressed by the strategic plan
9. Details of the strategic plan: tactics stretching out over 3–4 years if necessary, including progress milestones.

It is important to do things in the right order. For example, stating the future needs (step 3) before doing the market analysis (step 6) ensures that the requirements are ambitious and truly reflect what the business requires of the supply market, rather than being market-oriented and possibly scaled down by what we believe the supply limitations may be in future. Putting the latter first means that we accept what is on offer – putting ourselves first defines how we have to influence the market to work to our advantage. Also there is more to stating the needs than just forecasting volume, quality and delivery requirements. These may be termed the 'needs of the process' which will consume the materials/services being acquired. But there are also the 'needs of the business'. Two examples could be the need to keep abreast of new technology developments and the need to be able to predict gross margin with high confidence, the latter being especially relevant for significant price-volatile raw materials.

None of this is easy. The data to describe company-wide usage can be hard to get. The analysis takes a lot of time. The positioning statements are hard to write. Brevity is one challenge. Winston S. Churchill whilst away from his family and writing to them is credited with having said 'please excuse this long letter, but I have not had enough time to write a short one . . .'. Another reason why the positioning statements don't come easily is that some procurement people, expert as they are at their work, find it difficult to phrase things in the language of the boardroom. Here are real-life examples (concerning another raw material 'TBP') of a 'current' and a 'future' position statement which speak the language of the business rather than that of the procurement specialist.

The way it is now

Company profit and market share are heavily dependent on an increasingly expensive raw material for which there is no acceptable alternative. There are only two suppliers, both of whom make it specially for us. Profit and market share *and* future growth are exposed to limited availability, collusion between the suppliers on pricing, and the fact that at least one of the suppliers may not wish us to be their customer long term.

The way we want it to be

A secure expandable supply of TBP at a cost that will ensure product profitability now and in the future

---

Why 'nice' strategies

This is a mnemonic to help ensure that the strategy goal statement contains four essential ingredients:

1. The **Need**
2. The **Image** we wish to promote and achieve in the supply market, as a customer, in the course of implementing the strategy
3. The **Contribution** we wish to make to company financial performance over and above 'just' satisfying the need
4. The way in which we wish to manage the **Exposure** of our business to the supply market

'NICE' can be seen at work in the previous goal statements for raw materials 'X' and 'TBP' respectively:

	'X'	'TBP'
Need	responsive supply of (stating volumes, quality, etc.)	supply of (volumes, etc.)
Image	supply market which we influence	suppliers motivated
Contribution	advantageous price	cost competitiveness
Exposure	secure supply and non-volatile competitive pricing	supply security from sources who collaborate with us, not themselves'

The 'NICE' device is not rocket science, but still helpful!

The tools and process to use

In practice, at least half the time spent on strategy planning will be devoted to a detailed analysis of the current and future situations (step 6). At this stage a wide range of tools and techniques are deployed, of which the three most powerful for analysing 'today' are Supply Positioning, Vulnerability Analysis and Supplier Preference Overview. These are described more fully in chapter 11. The analysis will be the poorer without these and other techniques being used: data just stay as data and do not begin to tell a story. Using the tools turns data into intelligence. It also stimulates the data-capture process and it is common for participants in the strategy session to surprise themselves when they discover just how much they do know about suppliers, markets, supply chains, etc. It is easy to be confused by the fog of data; analytical tools clear the air and provide the visibility needed for forward thinking.

It is tempting now to construct a flow chart showing exactly what tools are used, and when. But to do so creates rigidities and begins to obscure why they are being used. The following diagram illustrates how the tools can be laid out and then brought into play as appropriate to the stage reached in the *upstream planning process* – 'upstream' being defined as all points in the procurement process up to and including commitment.

| **Supply planning** |

    | **Identify requirement** |

        | **Contract strategy** |

            | **Supplier selection** |

                | **Finalise contract** |

The precise purpose of each step was described in chapter 8. The key concept is that the stages are not sequential, but overlapping. It may be necessary, for example, to enter the 'select supplier' phase early with a first approach to suppliers to test their interest, the information gleaned then being ploughed back into 'supply planning'. The traditional buyer's job was to be expert at using specialist techniques, often in isolation, and always assuming the time was available to do it in the first place. In future the role demands more, such as the the ability to provide process leadership and facilitation of the multi-specialist strategy planning session.

Thus we see the buyer as 'conductor', orchestrating the strategic planning performance. But it is difficult to write a procedure about 'how to be good at process facilitation'. A brilliant violinist gets that way through a combination of believing it is important, learning from others, experience and practice – not by reading the Stradivarius instruction book. The best advice that can be given here is:

1. **Get the multi-specialist team involved from the outset**: you need their knowledge from the start, and the bonus is that this involvement also gets their commitment to the eventual action.
2. **Appoint someone as process leader:** analysis paralysis is likely without this.
3. **Allow sufficient time:** both overall and allocated between the key phases of the planning meeting – **days** if necessary.
4. If, and only if, it is absolutely impossible to get the time for strategy preparation

now, then **use the 'FASTRACK' approach** (see appendix). This is *not* a substitute for proper strategic planning, but it *is* better than nothing.

■ Appendix: Strategic procurement planning: 'Fastrack' strategy development

The 'FASTRACK' approach is a 'first strike' at preparing the strategic plan. At best it is a contingency measure, pending the time when a detailed acquisition plan is prepared by a multi-specialist cross-business team.

1. **Specification of need**
   Generic: 'Our business requires . . .'
   Specific

2. **Supply position**

   Exposure
   (a) No. sources available
   (b) No. sources acceptable
   (c) No. sources used
   (d) Cartel? Yes/No/Suspected
   (e) Demand: last year
                 now
                 future

   Profit/value
   (a) Contract value:
   (b) Expenditure/yr. on this item:
   (c) (b) as % of company total expend.:
   (d) Potential savings: %
   (e) Market trends impacting on cost?
       – raw materials pricing
       – supply surplus or shortage
       – technology change

   (f) Supply capacity: tight/balanced/surplus
   (g) External constraints? Yes/No
   (h) No. of sources: rising/stable/falling
   (i) Prices: rising/stable/falling
   (j) Specification: unique/standard?
   (k) Item part of our own output? Yes/No
   (l) Inventory costs: high/low
   (m) Current supplier performance: good/bad
   (n) Our spend as percentage of supplier T/O
   (o) Product position in life cycle:
       entrant/growth/stable/decline
   (p) Impact of non-supply: shutdown/
       lost revenue/off-quality/delay

   Vulnerabilities

   1. Dependence of business profitability on this supply: high
                       medium
                       low
                       none
   2. What can go wrong which will interrupt supply, damage quality, add cost?
      –
      –
      –
      –

Assessment of supply position

Strategic Security		Strategic-Critical	
	Tactical-Acquisition		Tactical Profit

3. **Supplier preference**, 'initial feel': Nuisance/Exploit/Develop/ Care
4. **Current situation**: Happy with it? If not, list specific reasons why not:

5. Describe how you would recognise **the future state** which, if it exists, would mean that current 'dis-satisfactions' disappear and potential opportunities are grasped:

6. Define your **strategic goal** in one or two sentences using the '*NICE*' formula: (*N*eed; *I*mage you want in supply market; *C*ontribution; *E*xposure being reduced)

7. Select **key elements of strategy** which will take us to the 'future state':

   ■ Exposure and vulnerability management by:
     – control of commercial exposure during early stage of procurement process
     – enhancement of contract strategy and/or contractual and performance controls
     – procurement marketing/improving supplier performance
     – creating competition by reverse marketing/wider sourcing/specification changes
         – split sourcing
         – contingency planning
         – in-sourcing or out-sourcing
         – other

   ■ Enhancement of profit and/or competitive advantage by:
     – building leverage through
         – market intelligence and/or supplier intelligence
         – consolidation of requirements (inside and/or ex-company)
     – building relationships with selected supplier(s) for cost reduction and/or innovation
     – other
8. Anticipating **the next negotiation**, what targets are you setting which will address today's need as well as move you in the direction your strategy requires:

Note: **A final reminder:** the 'FASTRACK' is intended to catalyse the process of 'first-level' strategic planning. It is *not* a substitute for proper planning (conducted as a structured, multi-specialist process) neither does it cover all the issues needing to be addressed. **But it is better than nothing!**

Chapter eleven

The strategic planning tool kit

High-performing procurement teams focus their effort on 'upstream' activity before contract award, activities such as supply market development, collaborating with internal users to develop new specifications, and understanding and influencing the way key suppliers run their businesses. But not every acquisition is treated in the same way: some have significantly more importance for the buyer's company, or the supply market may be seriously distorted as in the case of monopolies or cartels. And assuming that it is only the high-value contracts which are the most important ones overlooks the fact that a low-value item, if unavailable or defective, can make a huge negative impact on the operability or profitability of the customer company. The weak link that breaks the supply chain.

Three primary tools are available to address issues such as these: Supply Positioning, Supplier Preference Overview and Vulnerability Analysis. They are applied during the first stage in the upstream management of the procurement process, namely *Supply Planning*: the purpose of which is 'to ensure the existence of a supply market to which we have access and which enables us to succeed as a business both now and in future'. The Upstream Management stages were discussed in more detail in chapter 8, and these and the analytical tools are also presented fully in Court and Steele (1996).

▪ Supply positioning: opening windows on the supply market

The supply-positioning tool is used to assess supply criticality, and then to identify the overall goal of the supply management strategy. The items (materials, services, knowledge, etc.) required by a company to be in business are positioned on a two-axis grid depending on the degree to which there is a high or low dependence or exposure to the supply market (vertical axis), and also the relative contract value (horizontal axis). Consider products which are readily available, can be substituted, are on offer from several suppliers, are not technically complex, etc. These will be plotted low on the 'exposure' axis. But if the number of available suppliers is low, quality and other requirements become more demanding and the acquisition becomes more subject to external constraints (e.g. legislation), then items will move higher up the exposure axis. Low-value items will be placed towards the left end of the horizontal axis, but will move to the right with increasing value or increasing potential to make a major cost saving. The chart is then divided into four boxes, or categories. The supply management goal will then vary substantially depending on the category (see figure 11.1).

The *Tactical acquisition* box, contains low-value items available from many suppliers, but none of them crucial to the ongoing performance of the business. They are needed, but none are critical. The strategic goal is to minimise the involvement (and thus internal costs) of satisfying these needs. Several options are available, including the establishment of call-off contracts, delegation of commitment authority to users and 'procurement cards'.

Tactical profit items, high-cost requirements available from several competing suppliers, will respond to quick, sound judgements in the market-place. Typically they are readily available and provide the opportunity to reduce costs by careful use of competition and trading skills. The strategic goal is to maximise profit or value-for-money, and planning will focus on understanding movements and price trends in the market and correctly timing entry into it.

The *Strategic security* box contains low-value (but sometimes high-volume/low-unit-cost) items with few suppliers, or involving major quality, safety or environmental issues. Although their cost may be low, production will stop without them. The strategic aim is to ensure supply security and quality.

Strategic critical items combine high cost and high supply-side exposure. They are critical to the company's profitability and competitive advantage and must be kept under the closest scrutiny at all times. In addition, strategy will focus on influencing supply performance and on contingency planning. Relationship management will be a key priority. The strategic goal is closest possible supply and supplier management.

Supply Positioning is thus a powerful tool for selecting the overall strategic goal and has further advantages in that it also answers questions such as: 'How best to position supplier relationships. What skills do buyers need? What is appropriate for measuring purchasing performance?' It also has the power to open up non-buyers' awareness that procurement activity concerns external risk management and not just cost reduction. In fact, risk management is the first priority. The opportunity of pushing for cost reduction presupposes that a source exists and wants to supply you in the first place.

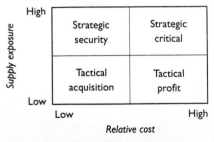

Figure 11.1 Supply positioning

■ Supplier preference overview: the view from the supply side

Powerful as it is, supply positioning is only half the story . . . it is the view of the supply market from the customer's perspective. What of the supplier's view? Whilst it may be that one in ten customer companies are acquainted with supply positioning, fewer than one in a hundred procurement departments are aware that suppliers use a similar technique to differentiate the importance of, and approaches to, different classes of customer.

This is a rude awakening for the buyer who has assumed that being in the position of having money to spend automatically puts them in the driving seat and makes them attractive to suppliers. But what if the buyer unintentionally makes life difficult for the supplier in a number of ways, for example by insisting on special treatment, by wanting to 'customise' an otherwise standard product, by making too many calls on the supplier's time for non-critical meetings or reporting routines, by being the 'last' customer for a product which comes off a production line which the supplier wishes to close? All such issues contribute to the supplier's cost of supply, eroding their profit margin. Couple them with the fact that the customer may not a big one, seldom pays on time, and keeps trying out alternative sources, and you have the makings of a situation where the supplier may actively plan to terminate the supply. And this will not necessarily be done by cancelling the contract, but perhaps through exploiting the situation by imposing big price increases.

The window through which the supplier looks to size up the customer is the Supplier preference overview. In this technique the supplier assesses the true cost and therefore profitability of doing business with a particular customer for a specified product or service. As well as the direct costs of production, all other costs incurred in winning and retaining the business are calculated and summed. These costs will include overheads' share, sales visits, etc. Other attractions that the customer may have for the supplier are also included in the equation. For example, a 'prestige' company may be one the supplier wishes to have on their client list for reference or credibility purposes. All these factors lead to a view about the 'attractiveness of the account' – high, low or in-between – to be shown on the vertical axis of another four-box grid (figure 11.2).

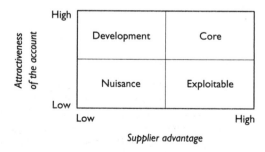

Figure 11.2 Supplier preference overview

The supplier then assesses the advantageousness of their position *vis-à-vis* the particular customer. Partly this reflects the relative value of the business in terms of sales revenue. But it also takes account of how well they 'have a foot in the door'. Are they a favoured source (high advantage)?, or Are there other supply competitors who have a bigger share of that customer's business and who perhaps have 'partnership' status with them (low advantage)? Supplier advantage is plotted on the horizontal axis.

The supplier now has quite different views of the customer, ranging from their being core to the supplier's business . . . to being an outright nuisance. Taking these two extremes, the supplier's stance will be respectively to give 'core' customers the highest level of service and to defend vigorously their position . . . whilst 'nuisances' will receive little attention and, if this leads to a loss of the customer, then that would be regarded as good rather than bad news. Discussions with 'development' customers will focus on expanding the business and identifying new opportunities, whilst 'exploitable' targets can expect large price increases, even if this means the supplier risking loss of the contract.

Adding one on one: the 'promised land', or Armageddon?!

The full power, and need, for applying supply positioning *and* supplier preference overview is demonstrated when the analyses are 'overlaid'. For example, it is good news if a Strategic Critical need is sourced from a supplier who sees the customer as 'core', but it could be 'the end of our world' if the supplier sees us as a nuisance. A positive overlap means that both sides will be devoting senior management priority and personal efforts into managing relationships between the two firms. Synergy and a mutual recognition that 'together we can do things which neither of us can do alone' will provide the bonding which keeps the parties together. If there is no overlap it is probably wise to assume that nothing can come from the relationship and to start contingency planning immediately. Short term this could mean building stocks, longer term it could mean 'make' rather than buy: changing specifications to create avenues to new sources, or to 'reverse market' (see later) new suppliers into existence.

But still the analysis has not gone far enough. The supply chain may still have weak links waiting to break and bring things to a halt. So now we need *vulnerability analysis*.

■ Vulnerability analysis

One of the primary aims of strategic procurement is to ensure the continued existence of, and access to, a supply market which forms the bedrock for the business overall. This is consistent with procurement's role to create a high-value low-cost supply base upon which the business can build successfully. This means ensuring supply security irrespective of the forces operating in the wider external environment. Fires, earthquakes, strikes, boats sinking, etc. are not acceptable excuses for an enterprise to be badly hurt by failed supply lines. But the chances of failure have to be assessed in addition to identifying what might go wrong. Vulnerability analysis does this.

Table 11.1 Vulnerability analysis

Potential Vulnerability	Probability	Likely Duration	Business Impact	Priority and Action

The first step is to map out the supply lines connecting you with the immediate source . . . then do the same for their sources and if necessary their sources' sources. The internal supply lines must be included as well, for example the supplier's manufacturing or service delivery process, storage arrangements, inherent operational hazards. And do not miss the human angle: the industrial relations' mood, possible turnover of key staff, etc., all can affect a critical supply if they go wrong. These are the 'potential vulnerabilities' (see table 11.1).

It is then necessary to assign a probability to their occurrence, the likely duration of the problem and the impact on our business should the event materialise. It is often then self-apparent what the priority areas are for corrective action and what the actions should be. In practice the analysis is easier to do than the description may imply. Two key hints are to avoid analysis-paralysis which happens if trying to calculate things to 'three places of decimals', and to conduct the analysis in a brainstorming environment with a multi-specialist, and if necessary cross-business, team.

■ So we've analysed the way it is: what next?

To complete the analysis of 'today's' situation is not to end but to begin the strategic planning process. Analysis is a waste of time if nothing is done with the output, and this in turn is not consistent with the core belief underlying the concept of strategic procurement: 'that the buyer will influence the supply market, rather than just accept it the way it is'.

A wide range of decision-making techniques, analytical tools and action options are now available to the buyer. Logical and tempting as it is, one has again to resist the temptation to link these rigidly together in the form of a decision tree. Too many decision trees makes it impossible to see the wood. But, more damaging, is that doing this suggests that strategic planning can be mechanised – even an activity flow-chart (extensive as it would be) would begin to put boxes around the thinking process and, in the worst case, provide procedural walls within which to audit buyer compliance. Composers do not present their music in the form of written procedures. Yes, they do set out the notes which have to be played, but the score is more pictorial than procedural and gives the conductor considerable latitude to interpret how things should happen, what resources might be used and when they should be brought in. So we are looking for a means of orchestrating the strategic planning process rather than defining it to the last detail. This idea was introduced in chapter 8 and can now be developed in more detail.

Figure 11.3 lays out the instruments available for use in the Upstream Management process and suggests where these may best be brought in. But exactly when is at the discretion of the conductor leading the performance. Do not be shut in by thinking certain tools must only be used where the diagram positions them in the planning phase: the intention is to illustrate what tools are available and their most likely position of use. Abbreviations in the boxes are the labels for the tools available. SP (Supply Positioning), VA (Vulnerability Analysis) and SPO (Supplier Preference Overview) have already been described, and shorter descriptions of the others follow now in alphabetical order:

AVIP: Affirmative Vendor Improvement Programmes These programmes comprise a number of options whereby the buyer works with the supplier to improve supply performance. The approach starts with the buyer targeting the supplier with whom it is appropriate to work, the next step often then being to put a performance measurement system in place. Performance improves and costs reduce as problems surface and are dealt with in a collaborative way. The supplier is made to feel '**A V**ery **I**mportant **P**art' of the customer's business. Benefits for the customer are obvious, but in addition they may well achieve a new level of 'supplier loyalty' and preferential treatment as a consequence of taking the trouble to work with the supplier in the first place. There is also a positive spin-off for the supplier in that their own competitiveness improves, resulting in winning orders from other customers which they may well have lost before.

B/N: Bid versus Negotiate Matrix With this tool the buyer analyses certain characteristics of the supply market and the item required and then makes an objective decision whether to seek competitive bids from potential suppliers, or to conduct parallel negotiations with them. Using this tool presupposes that a best-practice set of policies is in place which empowers buyers to be flexible in choosing how to approach the supply market (see SCS).

CA: Competitive Advantage Matrix A technique for assessing whether it is the buyer or the seller who has the stronger or weaker position in any given situation. Using it, buyers often find that they have a better case than they first thought. The outcome will determine what prominence, or otherwise, should be given to the specific elements in the deal being set up (e.g. price, contract duration, etc.).

CDT: Contract Decision Tree A tool for finding the right way through the contract and sub-contract maze to ensure that the specific type(s) of contract proposed is not only robust in its own right but is also compatible with other contracts which may also be in play. The emphasis is not so much on the legal integrity of the contract and its clauses, but on the overall framework of control that is established given the nature of the work, the different suppliers who may be involved and the expected behaviour of the supply market.

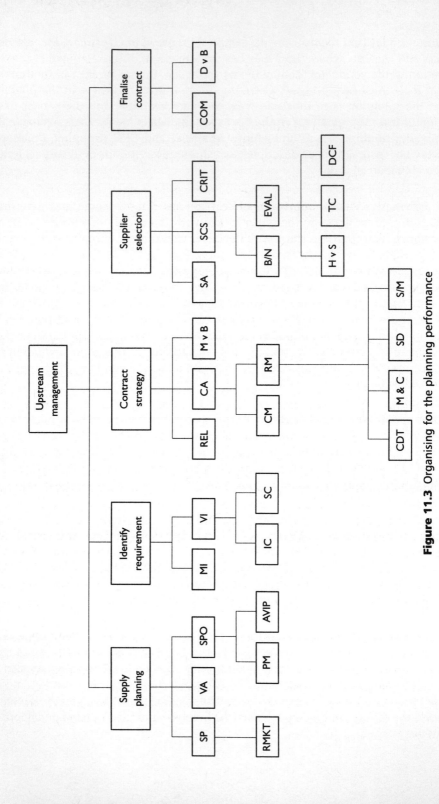

Figure 11.3 Organising for the planning performance

CM: Cost Modelling A systematic process of defining and quantifying the elements which make up the supplier's total cost in order to assess what pricing policy is being used and to test the integrity of the logic involved. Purchase price and cost analysis are included in cost modelling.

CRIT: Evaluation Criteria This technique defines the criteria, and threshold values, against which the acceptability of different supplier offers will be measured. The criteria must be established independently of the evaluation activity and before offers are received in order to avoid the criteria setting being influenced and perhaps compromised by early sight of what suppliers are offering. For critical requirements, and especially those where it may be necessary to develop supplier capability which is not currently available, the technique extends to include specific 'order-winning' criteria over and above the basic evaluation measures.

COM: Commitment Process This defines how the final approval of the supplier selection is obtained and what approach will be used to notify the successful supplier(s) and formally commit to a contract with them.

DCF: Discounted Cash Flow This is a financial analysis technique which enables up-front prices, other immediate costs, and future costs incurred during the lifetime of using the item or service being acquired to be summed in present-value terms. It is used in conjunction with the total cost approach and is essential if different supplier offers (e.g. containing different proposals for the phasing of payments) are to be compared on a like-for-like basis.

DeB: Debriefing of Unsuccessful Suppliers At face value this looks like a courtesy, assuming it is thought worthwhile doing anything at all. However it has its place as a technique in strategic procurement since, if done properly, it can motivate suppliers who have not won this time to do so in future. Commercially it is a sensitive process carrying the possibility of breaching confidences and creating mistrust. Done well, however, it is an instrument for maintaining and developing competitive alternatives for the future.

E: Evaluation of Offers This process comprises the techniques involved in bringing the different offers received from different suppliers to the same basis for comparison.

HvS: Hard versus Soft Money Hard money factors are easily quantifiable in money terms: price, discounts, payment terms, etc. are examples. Soft money factors do have a value but this is often more 'felt' than calculated. Examples are 'supplier expertise', 'technical support', 'knowledge of our procedures because they have worked for us before', etc. The hard versus soft money technique uses a mathematical discipline to convert 'soft' issues into hard money, thereby enabling objective comparisons to be made between competing offers.

IC: Interest Cycling The interest that a supplier has in a customer varies as the procurement process progresses. High interest in the early discussion phases reflects high supplier need for the order (and hence high buyer influence over the seller) but this can be replaced by dramatically lower interest levels once the order is captured – just when the customer has committed to the supplier and needs their full attention in fulfilling their obligations. Buyers who know about interest cycling will not just be maximising supplier interest after order placement (maybe by commencing well-timed discussions about possible new business) but will also be ensuring that 'buying signals' are not leaking out to the supplier early on in the procurement process. When this happens sellers become more certain of their chance of winning the order, the buyer losing leverage as a consequence.

M&C: Monopolies and Cartels A range of options for evaluating and dealing with market distortions. This part of the tool-kit includes a menu of alternatives for dealing with monopoly suppliers, and for recognising and circumventing cartels.

MI: Market Intelligence An area of activity which requires buyers to spend considerable time out in the market rather than at their desks. Intelligence is available from a wide range of external sources and also internally, in the minds of colleagues in other functions. This is one reason why a multi-functional (sometimes cross-business) team is essential at key stages in the strategic planning activity. Intelligence gathering is helped by having tools designed to facilitate the process (e.g. the FASTRACK approach).

MvB: Make versus Buy A decision framework within which the customer firm decides whether existing sources present sufficient security of supply for critical needs, or whether the required confidence can only be achieved by making in house – maybe taking over a supply company as the means of doing this. Supply security is not the sole consideration: proprietary designs or information security issues may also be present. Not least, making versus buying is a form of vertical integration and may therefore also be considered as a corporate strategy for securing competitive advantage over rival companies and a position from which to create leverage.

PM: Procurement Marketing Here the customer company actively 'markets' the benefits that it can offer to a supplier, over and above having a potential contract to place. A proven track record of helping suppliers to improve their performance, or bills being paid on time, are just two examples, but they only work if they are of value to the supplier. The buyer therefore needs to do homework first in order to get a good 'fix' on the needs that the supplier has which the buyer may satisfy. Procurement marketing is used when it is desired to increase supplier interest in the customer, the premise being that the more the supplier is interested the more influence or leverage the buyer possesses.

REL: Relationship Positioning The object is to determine what type of buyer–seller relationship will best serve the buyer's needs. This will be significantly influenced by the output from SP and SPO. Detailed analysis tools will be used to decide where in the relationship spectrum – from arms length to close collaboration – it will be best to be.

RM: Risk Management The overall process of identifying the ways in which the customer company operations and profitability are exposed to supply market risks (e.g. supplier failure, being exploited by price-fixing) and then acting to reduce or nullify them.

RMKT: Reverse Marketing A concept pioneered by Professors Michiel R. Leenders and David L. Blenkhorn and described fully in their excellent book 'Reverse Marketing' (Leenders and Blenkhorn, 1988). This strategy reverses the traditional supplier–buyer relationship in that the buyer sets out to create 'good, better and exceptional suppliers' where none may presently exist. The deliverables include increased supply security, dramatic cost reduction and competitive advantage in that the customer company stands to benefit where its competitors do not.

SA: Supplier Appraisal In most companies this is a well-organised set of techniques and measures available for testing suppliers' capabilities to meet all the performance criteria deemed to be important by the customer company as regards supplier performance. For critical needs and intended longer relationships the assessment extends to include the viability of the supplier as a business overall and the values and philosophies which guide their decision-making and behaviour.

SC: Supplier Conditioning Here the buyer will be using tactics to channel or 'condition' the supplier's thoughts in the way the buyer wishes them to go. For example, supplier's expectations of achieving a price increase can be reversed by early and skilful propaganda from the customer side on the need, logic and benefits of agreeing reductions instead.

SCS: Search for Competitive Source(s) In a best-practice procurement environment, SCS makes available a range of 'procurement tactics' which enable the buyer to be selective in choosing the optimum way of approaching suppliers for offers, given the prevailing conditions in the supply market and longer-term procurement goals. A key policy will be in place whereby the acceptability of an offer will be judged according to its total value and its compatibility with strategic aims. In a less-than-best-practice scenario buyers are required always to use a stipulated procurement tactic (e.g. seek formal tenders) regardless of circumstances, and 'lowest price' will be the selection yardstick.

SD: Source Dependency This is a framework within which to decide the maximum extent to which the buyer wishes to depend on one source for an important requirement. Considerations include the impact of supplier failure if the customer has 'too many eggs in the one basket' and the impact on the supplier's business if the customer has a large order which is taken away. The focus is on the one supplier who is involved rather than how to split the business between two or more (see S/M).

customer has a large order which is taken away. The focus is on the one supplier who is involved rather than how to split the business between two or more (see S/M).

S/M: Single/Multiple Sourcing This tool helps to decide the optimum split of business between two or more suppliers. Considerations include the degree to which supply security is a priority and the impact on other suppliers (and thus on competitive pricing levels) if too much business is given to one supplier for too long.

SP: Supply Positioning A primary analytical tool for determining the strategic importance to the customer of the items/materials/services, etc. acquired from the supply market to meet the needs of the business. Categorising these items sets the priorities for the buyer and also defines the overall strategic goal and acquisition tactics appropriate to the importance of the item concerned.

SPO: Supplier Preference Overview A primary analytical tool for assessing how the customer might look from the supplier's viewpoint. The result may be that the supplier sees the customer as core to their business, a nuisance to be dropped at the earliest opportunity or something in-between. The buyer then looks for compatibility between this conclusion and that required by supply positioning. If there is a disconnect, then urgent actions, starting with contingency planning, are required.

TC: Total Cost This tool facilitates the calculation of total lifetime costs of a supplier proposal as distinct from looking only at the price offered. Its use is necessary because total costs may exceed a budget amount whereas price alone may come within it. It also has to be recognised that some suppliers use a low-price order-getting approach to win business and then rely on charging subsequent costs as their source of profit from the job.

VA: Vulnerability Analysis A primary tool used to identify weak links in the supply chain and then to assess the probability and impact of their failing. The tool then highlights the priority areas for corrective action.

VI: Vendor Intelligence Different from general market intelligence which focusses on overall trends, availability, competitor activity, etc., vendor intelligence focusses on a supply company as a business entity. Its strategic goals, current performance, ownership, in-house developments, salesperson track record, etc. are examples of areas to probe. The aim is to build influence and leverage through a deep understanding of what it is that drives supplier decision-making, both corporately and individually at the salesperson level. The process of gathering vendor intelligence is facilitated by the use of checklists, and using technical visits to the supplier as a means of working simultaneously to a (concealed) commercial agenda.

■ Instruments are for playing tunes . . . not making notes

Using tools in a rigid and mechanistic way will not produce a good strategic plan. The sound of strategic procurement comes from people orchestrating their efforts for a common purpose, using the instruments and their expertise in a flexible and appropriate way. It is not 'note-bashing', one after another, without a discernible theme emerging. It is for this reason that we are not concerned if the boxes containing the strategic planning tools may not, as shown in figure 11.3, be connected together quite right. They are not 'hard-wired' together anyway and, besides, the five key phases of upstream management are not sequential steps independent of each other, but more a flow of activity where jumping ahead and then recycling is not just permitted but actually necessary. For example, supply positioning may point to the need for a close relationship with a unique supplier but who, when tested, however, cannot or will not subscribe to the attitude and performance requirements specified by the 'relationship positioning tool': which in turn means recycling back to 'reverse marketing' as needing to be a feature of the strategic plan to create a supplier who does meet the criteria.

Nor does it matter that some of the 'tools' seem to be not tools but activities, especially as the procurement process moves towards finalising the contract. Strategic Planning belongs more to the left of the figure 11.3 layout and operational activity to the right. Debriefing unsuccessful suppliers is an example of an activity rather than a tool. Operational in nature and seemingly only to do with tidying up after striking a deal with someone else, it needs to be thought about much earlier in the planning process since it may be a crucial step towards the longer-term goal of creating more contenders for our business in future. This is the essence of strategic procurement: to operate in the supply market now such that we do not just set up deals for today but in the process move towards creating a supply market which will be better for us tomorrow. We want our instrumentalists to create the definitive performance, not merely to engage in the mechanics of making notes.

■ References

Court, Brian and Paul Steele (1996) *Profitable Purchasing Strategies*, Berkshire: McGraw-Hill Book Company.

Leenders, Michiel R. and David L. Blenkhorn (1988) *Reverse Marketing: The New Buyer-Seller Relationship*, New York: The Free Press.

Chapter twelve

Managing the supply interface – ten key questions

The aim of this chapter is to provide a comprehensive overview of all the issues relevant to 'managing the supplier interface'. Overall, the topic is a microcosm of all that is involved in the functional aspects of procurement activity. The chapter alone could form a whole book in its own right but, in the interests of brevity, we'll deal only with those topics which are not covered in detail elsewhere.

Chapters 10 and 11 dealt with preparing strategy. Now it is time to think closely about which suppliers are likely to be appropriate as parties to the strategy. 'Supply-planning' activities will have focussed on issues such as the degree to which the customer will or will not be dependent on the supplier and what sort of responses are needed from the supplier, consistent with the needs of the strategy.

Now we look at the supplier side of the equation. The view spans ten key questions about supplier relationships.

1. Where are they?
2. How do we appear to them – and are they interested?
3. Will they be any good?
4. Who will be the main contact between our companies?
5. How important are they and their supplies to us?
6. How should we approach them?
7. How might we be tied together?
8. With whom do we contact – and is it the best deal?
9. How do we keep them under control?
10. Was it OK?

The best companies consider *all* the following as relevant, but the degree to which each is developed and applied depends on the supply criticality of each case in question.

■ 1. Suppliers – where are they?

Most companies keep a data-base of suitable suppliers. This is usually the buyer's first port of call when putting together a short-list of suppliers who might be invited to make offers to satisfy the customer's need. The data may have started by being simply a collection of supplier brochures, but this usually evolves into a more formal list of suppliers who have been screened for acceptability (see 3 below) and who may have been used before.

Data-bases such as the above can only include suppliers that are already known about. But how are others discovered? One novel approach involves the customer producing a small brochure aimed at suppliers and inviting them to get in touch. As an 'image influencer' and door opener they are invaluable. However the search for new sources requires more than this, and lists other sources of information are as follows:

Internal company reports
Published journals
Newspapers and associated services
Informal contacts with suppliers, and the supplier personally
Visit to supplier's premises
Published company reports and financial accounts
Agencies providing specialist services, and published directories
Consultants and market-sector analysts
Contact with other buyers
Trade exhibitions, seminars, conferences, courses
Industry associations and sub-committees
Government departments and embassies
Supplier 'road shows'
Enquiry telexes and invitations to bid or tender
Information obtained during technical visits
Information obtained during negotiations
Colleagues in our company who have contacts with the supplier
Other contacts in the supply company (other than the salesperson)

■ 2. How do we appear to them . . . and are they interested?

First comes the issue of image. Here are some comments from some suppliers about certain customers:

- ■ 'technically they know just what they want, but they are predictable in approaching the supply market so we known their game plan before we even get started'
- ■ 'their market is growing so quickly they can't spend money fast enough. Add 15 per cent to the prices'
- ■ 'there's little challenge in selling to them – they even pay for us to correct the mistakes we might have made in the last order!'

Suppliers with these impressions are hardly going to put themselves out to excel for the customer, and the customer loses out in consequence. A customer company cannot *not* have an image: just by 'being there' it sends messages to others, good and bad. So it is important is to influence the eyes of the beholders and manage the image you wish them to see. And saying 'we're an important company so you'd better give us your best offer' will not necessarily obtain the best response. In most cases it is not the relative posturing which matters but the quality of the personal relationship between buyer and seller. *Companies* do not do deals with each other: *people* do.

A formula which seems to work is captured in the following image statement: 'We wish to project a tough, challenging, but fair image to suppliers which encourages them to be responsive, innovative and efficient in their supply of resources (materials or services) to us.'

Be selective though. Whilst *all* suppliers must be treated according to the basic rules of etiquette and ethical behaviour, it is only the 'strategic security' and 'strategic critical' sellers who need the full image treatment. You need them as much as (perhaps more than) they need you.

But are they interested?

Suppliers may have spare capacity with which to meet your needs but this doesn't automatically mean that they will want to. A lot depends on whether or not your custom fits in with what they regard as their core activity. And even if there *is* a strategic fit, maybe you will be positioned as a 'nuisance' customer because you repeatedly change your requirements or insist on special treatment.

For some time, suppliers have been using 'segmentation techniques' which label their customers into different categories. This determines the treatment the customer will receive. It can range from exploiting them by imposing dramatic price increases, through to cosseting them in order to sustain and develop a strategically important relationship. High-class buyers are now using similar techniques (one such being the Supplier Preference Overview) to 'second guess' the supplier's thinking about the relationship. Just as Supply Positioning provides a window through which the buyer can look out to determine the company's dependence on the supply market, so Supplier Preference Overview gives the complementary picture of the customer from the supplier's viewpoint.

Everything is fine when there is a 'fit' (e.g. a strategic critical item for the buyer comes from a supplier who sees the customer as strategically important), but start panicking when you realise that you are being positioned as a 'nuisance'. An immediate response would be to establish contingency plans to protect supply security but, longer term, additional tactics must be deployed. One such is 'Procurement Marketing', a planned approach designed to persuade the supplier of the benefits of 'us' as a customer. The buyer thus establishes more influence over the supplier and the balance of power is restored.

■ 3. Will they be any good?

Supplier appraisal is one of procurement's more widely accepted and traditional activities. Even so, many companies focus too much on assessing 'what' it is that the supplier makes and miss important issues to do with the capability and culture of the supply company overall. It is flawed to think that if we know everything there is to know about the product then we know all there is to know about the supplier. Nothing could be further from the truth, and the list below shows that a good appraisal process focusses not just on the product or service provided, but also on the organisation behind it, looking now *and* into the future:

Production facilities and environment
Production control and quality assurance
After-sales service
Reputation with other customers
Company organisation and ownership
Factory and office locations
Financial backing and liquidity or debt situation
Accounts details
Calibre and motivation of personnel
Design and development capability
Effectiveness of procurement team, process and supplier management activity
Effectiveness of management of sub-contract activity
Supply chain management effectiveness (external logistics and internal inventory management)
Macro-change programmes, e.g.:
  – world best-practice initiatives
  – corporate vision (if any)
  – goal of corporate strategy (if any)
In-house developments, e.g.:
  – office/factory relocation
  – systems developments
  – efficiency/cost-cutting initiatives
  – culture-change programmes?
  – implementation of 'new-management' thinking?
Assessment of how they might position us as a customer

The supplier appraisal process is best conducted as a cross-functional activity orchestrated by the procurement team.

■ 4. Who will be the main contact between our companies?

Contacts with the supply market need to be orchestrated and to take place according to certain policies. If this is not done then fragmentation and inconsistency occur and suppliers will be looking at a customer company which does not have its game together . . . making it an 'advantage supplier'. Just as sales teams are the primary links between a company and its customers, so procurement provides that role on the input side of the business. The key issue is that someone feels accountable for the proper conduct of these interactions. 'Orchestrating' the contacts does not mean that buyers are involved in every instant, but they do need to know that contacts are occurring and that behaviours are appropriate.

In addition to requirements for ethical behaviour, there are two particularly relevant best-practice policies which guide customer–supplier interactions. These are 'Company Image in the Supply Market' and 'Dealing with Supplier Visitors'. Image has been discussed above. A policy statement (in italics below) for Supplier Visitors, together with descriptive context, may be expressed as follows:

> Many different people in our company, at all levels, will be visited by supplier visitors and it is likely that the majority of these visits will be with non-procurement personnel. This creates a commercial exposure for us in that, if our company colleagues are not able to recognise and handle subtle sales approaches, then it is likely that commercially sensitive information will be released. *Company personnel may freely meet with supplier visitors, but must be aware of the tactics used by sellers to obtain and plant information, and must be guarded about releasing information which can lose commercial advantage for our company. Personnel who do not possess commitment authority must neither commit the company nor give the impression that a contract has been or will be awarded.*

Whilst this reflects current thinking on best practice, it is up to the procurement manager to decide whether his or her company is ready for this policy at this time. In one company the director is so concerned at the current 'out of control' situation that, for the time being, the policy is that no contacts with suppliers may take place without buyer participation. Not a sustainable position in the longer term, but a necessary way of managing the commercial exposure which exists 'today'.

■ 5. How important are they, and their suppliers, to us?

The natural way of deciding on procurement priorities is to spend more time on the high-value items, less on the low. But there are two problems with this approach. First is that, despite the good intentions, the volume of low value transactions is often so high as to consume most of the buyer's time. Table 12.1 shows how the order-value distribution works out in one company.

The distortion is remarkable. For example, taking all contracts up to $7,500 as a group, the total of all these transactions is 1,553 (87.5 per cent of the total) yet the amount expended is just $2.17 million (14.3 per cent of the total spend). The average value of all the transactions in the $0–7,500 range is only $1,397. Putting it another way, 87.5 per cent of the total purchasing effort is spent dealing with orders having an average value of less than $1,500. But the problem is that these requests for purchasing action will not go away: somehow they have to be dealt with. Various options are available for reducing the need for direct attention (e.g. set up call-off orders for users to action when needed; contract out of the activity; give the user some buying authority; use procurement 'credit cards') but until these happen the buyer is sucked into the work.

Table 12.1 Real case: order–value distribution

Value range $'000		Number of Orders	Total value $ million	Value as % of total 'T'	Average order value, $
min	max				
0	0.15	212	0.02	0.1	94
0.15	0.75	615	0.25	1.7	407
0.75	1.50	275	0.30	2.0	1,091
1.50	**7.50**	**451**	**1.60**	**10.5**	**3,548**
7.50	75.00	208	4.40	29.0	21,154
>75.00		13	8.60	56.7	661,538
TOTAL		1,774	15.17 (= 'T')		

The second problem with the idea that 'importance depends on money spent' is that it ignores the matter of risk. A small-spend item may be vital for day-to-day operational reliability – without it nothing can be done, apart from apologising to customers for non-delivery. Risk or exposure can be set alongside the cost aspect using the two-dimensional Supply Positioning technique already described. Using this technique gives us the correct answer as to 'What is Important?'.

■ 6. How should we approach them?

The buyer is not yet ready to make any contracts because offers have not been received from possible suppliers, so question 6 addresses how best to obtain them. Offers may be invited in a number of ways, formally or informally. A supplier may be asked verbally to quote a price around which there may be subsequent negotiation, or the approach may be more structured by making a formal request to the supplier to submit a tender for the work. These options are referred to as 'purchase tactics' and the one to choose in any situation depends not just on the importance or complexity of the need but also on the state of the supply market. Less-than-good companies ignore the latter point and pay significantly higher prices – more than 30–50 per cent for example – as a result. A dire outcome such as this could arise in the event that cartels exist. The way to deal with distortions, i.e. uncompetitive market situations, such as this is discussed in chapter 14. The main answer to the question of how best to approach the supplier is first to establish a 'best-practice policy' framework which makes it possible for the buyer to choose from a range of opening moves or 'purchase tactics' depending on the buyer's reading of the prevailing market situation.

■ 7. How might we be tied together?

This relates to the many different types of orders and contracts available, ranging from spot orders to long-term deals and lump sum contracts to unit-rate arrangements. A contract decision tree helps to choose correctly. Supply Positioning will also give a lead. For instance, where lowest price *is* the focus and a competitive supply market is driving the best deal towards the customer, then a short-term fixed-price contract may be best. On the other hand, if cost-effective supply security is the goal then a long-term contract may provide the environment within which buyer and seller work together to remove costs from the supply arrangements with the benefits showing up as continually reducing unit rates: fewer 'units' and lower 'rates'.

It is also necessary to select the right form of supplier relationship. This may range from arm's-length to very close collaboration. Best practice is for the customer company to be selective about what is needed, keeping in mind that the relationship is a means to an end and not an end in itself. The not-so-good companies tend to operate continually at the extremes: every supplier is an adversary or, alternatively, a partner for life. Relationship options are examined in more detail in chapter 15.

■ 8. With whom do we contract . . . and is it the best deal?

Crunch time. Offers are on the table – but how to choose between them? The question has two parts:

- ■ How do we know the suppliers' offers are their best ones?
- ■ How do we choose which one to accept?

First, how best is best?

The same question could be asked of a salesperson or an industrial relations negotiator of the deals they conclude. And on the macro scale, how do we know the CEO is getting the best performance results from the company overall? If the answer was simple then computers could calculate it and we are saved from having to use management judgement to decide on strategic goals in the first place and then assessing the acceptability of the results achieved.

But perhaps we are asking the wrong question. In an age when organisations are striving to achieve competitive advantage over their rivals surely the object is to be better than them (which *is* measurable) rather than wasting effort trying to prove whether or not we have achieved the 'best' results possible. 'Looking for best' is likely to be a fruitless calculation anyway since by definition 'best possible' has not been achieved yet, by anyone, so we have nothing with which to compare actual results. In contrast to abstract calculations it is constantly doing things differently in search of 'best' that stimulates performance improvement which makes us better than the rest. As long as we are driving forward to do things significantly better than before and we are outperforming our competitors (both issues are measurable) then 'proving we are best' ceases to be relevant, especially as extrapolating towards 'best' from the data of past experience is likely to land well short of what is potentially possible.

So, if there is no easy one-line answer to the question 'have we got the best deal?' what we *can* say is:

1. that we actually did get a deal
2. that we avoided conditions which we know would have contributed to its being a bad deal
3. that the outcome meets or exceeds our goals, targets, budgets, etc. as we envisage them today
4. that the outcome is line with our strategy
5. maybe some other signs told us we that we got the best deal going, either at the time, or later

The following expands the above points in the order in which they are made:

1. Securing a deal is not automatic. Assuming it *will* be is to perpetuate the myth that 'suppliers always want to supply'. The reality is that suppliers more and more are choosing who they want to sell to. Your company may not be one of them.

2. Companies in which there is 'careless talk' (which unwittingly reveal commercial targets) between non-procurement personnel and suppliers, where buyers are hindered by rigid procedures, and where distorted supply markets are approached in a naive way . . . are asking for bad deals and will get them. Creating capability to deal with these commercial exposures sets the scene for achieving better results.

3. Assuming that the buying company's expenditure budgets and performance targets are linked closely to challenging corporate goals and that they represent real needs as opposed to aiming merely for incremental improvements on what the supply market chooses to offer: then meeting or exceeding these goals clearly contributes directly to corporate success.

4. This presupposes that there is a strategy. A good deal is one which fully meets today's needs. A 'best' deal is one which does that and also moves us towards a future goal.

5. Other signs may signal that the buyer has obtained the best deal available. A later chapter covers 'negotiation', and it is during this process that the skilled observer of non-verbal behaviour may see that the seller's 'walk-away' point, i.e. their best offer, has been reached. Subjective as this may be, it is a more reliable indicator than having the sellers reveal their targets to you after the event. And the practice of comparing prices with other customers for similar supplies is not going to reveal much of value either. Research shows that parties to such data-sharing schemes do not reveal their best prices, so the comparisons are misleading. On a higher level, some buyer–seller collaborations have delivered stunning results which represent a quantum leap ahead of what it was thought possible to predict at the outset. Truly best deals can only be recognised some time after the event.

   If the one-line question is 'how do we know we've got the best deal?', then the best one-line answer is 'because it is exactly in line with our strategy'. But make sure you have one!

How do we choose which deal to accept?

Evaluating and choosing between the different supplier offers brings a different challenge. In the simplest case, where offers from several excellent suppliers are genuinely competitive, where 'apples are compared with apples' and where there are no hidden cost factors to quantify, then perhaps it is only necessary to select on the basis of lowest price. More complex cases require the traditional skills of 'bid evaluation', including the use of time–value-of-money techniques. Their use is illustrated in figure 12.1. These techniques will not be discussed here since they are well covered in other business texts. But how do we assess the cost implications of judgemental matters to which it is difficult to attach costs? This is where the concept of 'hard money versus soft money' comes in. Table 12.2 gives examples.

Table 12.2 Hard money versus soft money aspects of a deal

Examples of hard money

    Price
    Volume discounts
    Payment terms
    Service charges
    Price variation formulae

Examples of soft money

    Expertise
    Previous experience of working with our company
    Trained/experienced manpower and management
    Technical back-up to support contract execution
    Attitudes to safety, total quality, etc.
    Ability to manage sub-contractors

Applied logic using Kepner-Tregoe techniques will translate soft money factors into hard money numbers which in turn are inserted into the arithmetical bid comparison. The appendix provides a worked example of the total cost-evaluation process used to select between two offers.

Awarding the contract

In signing the contract the customer's representative (at whatever level: buyer or CEO) is employing their delegated authority to act as their company's legal agent. This results in a valid and legally binding contract with the other party.

The manner in which successful and unsuccessful suppliers are advised of the outcome of the acquisition strategy and tactics has an important bearing on subsequent relationships between buyer and seller. The aim is to keep the successful supplier(s) motivated to deliver their best efforts throughout the contracting process and beyond. They will *not* do so if, for example, in the course of post-award discussions they feel they have been exploited into offering too much for too little. Also, by controlled

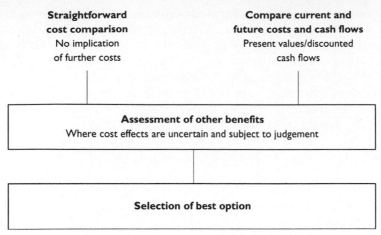

Figure 12.1 Comparison of alternative offers

debriefing, it is possible to maintain the interest of unsuccessful suppliers wanting to offer their services again in future. But they will *not* do this if they feel that the buyer never intended to take them or their offer seriously, or that customer expectations were and always will be beyond the supplier's capability to deliver.

The best rule is that, unless required by law, neither successful nor unsuccessful suppliers may be given *any* commercial information which will allow them to compare their offer with those of other suppliers who competed for the same business. However, as a result of being able to examine the technical, operational and commercial proposals of those suppliers participating in the procurement process the buyer will be in a position to counsel suppliers on how their offers can be further enhanced in future. Buyers, where they judge it to be appropriate, should discretely offer such advice to successful and unsuccessful suppliers, but *only* on the basis that confidentialities are not breached. The object is to improve the general performance level of all suppliers, not to give one an unfair competitive edge over the others.

■ 9. How do we keep them under control?

In all cases, other than once-off immediately fulfilled orders, it is necessary to ensure that proper controls are in place to govern the effectiveness of the commercial relationship as time goes on. Prices may rise uncontrollably, supplier performance may fall off, loopholes may be left which encourage fraud, and these topics are covered as follows:

- ■ price management (chapter 13)
- ■ abuse of contract loopholes (chapter 5)
- ■ supplier performance maintenance/improvement ((10) below and chapter 15)

Responsibilities during contract execution must be clearly defined. In order to optimise day-to-day interactions between customer and supplier it will normally be the user who handles supervision and operational administration of an order or contract after award. The best policy is that the user has primary responsibility for achieving a contract's intended purpose and also for advising when completion is satisfactorily achieved. On both issues users may liaise directly with suppliers but such communications must be limited to operational issues which can be handled within the framework of the contract. Buyers must be involved if it becomes necessary to change any aspects of the contract which impact on the commercial basis of the agreement, or if contractual safeguards have to be exercised. Changes and claims are particularly sensitive aspects of contract administration and buyers must be involved with both.

■ 10. Was it OK?

Monitoring of suppliers' performance during the contract period is required not just to ensure best performance 'now', but also to provide the basis for continual improvement in future. The criteria against which performance is rated will vary depending on the nature and criticality of the supply. One company's simplest approach involves just four weighted (weightings in brackets) categories: product acceptability (40 per cent), delivery (25 per cent), customer service (25 per cent), pricing (10 per cent). Where an in-depth rating is required, that same company's approach is more comprehensive as shown in table 12.3.

Table 12.3 Supplier performance measurement

DELIVERY
    Delivers on time
    Meets due date without expediting
    Competitive lead time
    Delivers proper items and quantities
    Provides accurate documentation and information
    Responds to emergency delivery requirements

PRICING
    Competitiveness
    Price stability
    Manner in which price changes (up and down) are introduced

CUSTOMER SERVICE
    Compliance with contract terms and conditions
    Supplier representatives have sincere desire to serve
    Provides feedback from factory/manufacturer
    Effectiveness of inside sales support
    Market insight
    Training provided on equipment or products

Support on professional/technical matters
Administrative efficiency (includes order acknowledgement and invoicing)
Adherence to their company policies

PRODUCT
Reliability/durability/meeting specifications
Documentation, instructions, technical manuals
Packaging, suitability, environmental aspects
Contract service quality

The idea is to monitor supplier performance in overall terms and not just compliance with the contract, and that there will be active interaction with the suppliers concerned in order to achieve continual improvement. The first criterion for success is that the assessment is a team activity and involves a selection of the people in the buyer's company who have dealings and contact with the supplier. Secondly, the supplier gets feedback – good and bad.

■ Appendix: 'Clean-up on costs': a total-cost-evaluation case study

An important piece of manufacturing plant maintenance equipment needs to be acquired for one of the sites of a major chemical company. The equipment is a high-tech water pressure-jet machine regularly used to clean the external surfaces of air-fin heat exchangers, all of which are some four metres above ground level. Previously there has been only one option acceptable to the technical specialists and this equipment has been provided by FRENDVEND Ltd, a valued supplier well known to the plant. In fact it is one of their machines that is now to be replaced.

Early technical discussions with FRENDVEND have identified their type-A machine as being most suitable. The list price of this equipment is $112,000 although it is unfortunate that the salesperson has managed to find out that the manufacturing people have budgeted $127,000 for the purchase. FRENDVEND advise that an additional 3 per cent of the list-price is payable on delivery to cover delivery and commissioning costs. Delivery is in 6 months' time but FRENDVEND want a down-payment of 50 per cent of the price now with the balance paid at delivery.

The pressure-jet machines run off electricity and even FRENDVEND's type-A machine will cost $1,000 per week to run. However the plant has a special arrangement with the utility company which means that each full year's electricity cost is paid at the end of each full year of operation. Costs are expected to rise 5 per cent annually.

Although you may once have been forced into a single-source situation for this equipment, things could improve since another supplier, FRESHSTART INC, has announced a new state-of-the-art cleaning machine. FRESHSTART is a well-established company of good reputation, and the industry is excited by the technical breakthrough represented by their machine. It relies on a low-pressure system which offers a 50 per cent energy saving compared with FRENDVEND's machine. However this is only possible because the water it uses is dosed with a proprietary chemical only available from FRESHSTART. A further advantage is that their equipment is fitted with an extendable arm which remotely positions the spray jets close to the air-fin exchanger surfaces. This eliminates the need for staging or scaffolding to get access to the exchangers (which is necessary with FRENDVEND's machine) and could yield some useful manpower savings compared with the current situation.

In response to your invitation, FRESHSTART have quoted a price of $163,000 for their machine, including delivery and commissioning. They seem keen to attract you as their first important customer for this machine and this is reflected in their requirement of only 10 per cent payment with order, with 90 per cent payable on delivery which is promised for six months' from order.

Based on the planned machine usage pattern (in service 52 weeks per year) you calculate that the chemical costs will be $100 per week. FRESHSTART's quote advises that a whole year's requirement for the chemical must be purchased and paid for at the start of each full year of machine usage, but the chemical's unit price is not expected to change in the foreseeable future. However the technical specialists are confident that an annual 5 per cent reduction in chemical consumption will be achieved as the plant operating personnel become more skilled in selecting the right dose rates. Another interesting feature of FRESHSTART's environmentally friendly design is that a large number of the machine components can be recycled at the end of the machine's life (three full years from the commissioning date). This means that, at that time, FRESHSTART guarantee to repay to the customer 30 per cent of the original price. In contrast, FRENDVEND would repay 5 per cent to preserve 'goodwill', but *only* if the customer intends at that time to purchase a new machine from them.

At first glance it is tempting to place your order with FRENDVEND since their price is well within budget (unless the salesman charges for 'extras') and you would be buying equipment with which the plant people already have experience. In addition, your analysis of FRESHSTART 'soft money' factors indicates that their price should be increased by 7 per cent as a contingency against any unexpected costs. You are also advised that a further $5,000 should be added to their bid to cover the costs of detailed technical evaluation, which anyway should perhaps be the next step which you recommend to be taken.

Tasks

1. How many total-cost components can you identify in the above scenario?

2. What is your estimate of the 'present value' of the total costs of the FRENDVEND and FRESHSTART options respectively?

Additional financial information

At your company's current cost of capital:

$1,000 in 6 months' time is worth $ 952 today
$1,000 in 9 months $ 929
$1,000 in 1 year $ 909
$1,000 in 18 months $ 865
$1,000 in 2 years $ 826
$1,000 in 30 months $ 786
$1,000 in 3 years $ 751
$1,000 in 42 months $ 715

■ Results

Task 1: Total cost components

Obvious:	Price	Payment phasing
	Delivery and commissioning costs	Energy consumption
	Energy price	Energy payment date
	Chemical consumption	Chemical payment date
	Technical checks	Realisation on equipment disposal
	Contingency	
Less Obvious:	Lead time	Rebate on existing machine (FRENDVEND)
	Chemical price (expected constant)	Chemical usage annually
Other Benefits:	Environmental politics and PR	
	Possible maintenance savings plus possible productivity deal	

Task 2: Calculation on present values

FRENDVEND: **Price:** 50% of $112,000 now   = $56,000
                        50% of $112,000 in 6 months   = $53,312
                        3% delivery/commissioning in 6 months = $ 3,199
                Energy: Yr1, $52,000 paid in 18 months = $44,980 ⎫
                        Yr2, $54,600   30   = $42,916 ⎬ $128,887
                        Yr3, $57,330   42   = $40,991 ⎭

                  Present value of total cost: $241,398

FRESHSTART: **Price:** 10 per cent of $163,000 now   = $ 16,300
                        90 per cent of $163,000 in 6 months = $139,658
                        Delivery/commissioning   included
                Energy: 50 per cent of FRENDVEND   = $64,444
                Chems: Yr1, $5,200 paid in 6 months   = $ 4,950
                        Yr2, $4,940   18   = $ 4,273
                        Yr3, $4,693   30   = $ 3,689

Contingency: 7% of $163,000 now	= $11,410
Technical evaluation:	= $ 5,000
Payback credit: 30% of $163,000 in 3.5 years	=($34,964)
Present value of total cost:	$214,760

Conclusion: FRESHSTART cost is $26,638 less (11 per cent)

Chapter thirteen

Getting around price

A salesman had quoted a price of $83,746 for a major potential order. In an off-guard moment he was heard to say to his sales colleague '$83,000 or thereabouts is what I think we can get the customer to pay, the 746 is for credibility'! The '746' does of course suggest that the price has been carefully worked out and not just plucked out of the air: but perhaps more powerfully it perpetuates the general assumption that all prices are based on costs. Detailed price lists, price-review formulae based on cost factors, evidence produced to support a requested price increase and other similar devices are also designed to convey the same impression. Why? Because it makes it difficult for the buyer to challenge prices. To do so would be to dispute the costing calculations, and maybe the buyer feels in a weak position to do this. Or the feeling may be that forcing a supplier to reduce price would erode the profit margin and cause them to make a loss. The consequent threat of driving the supplier out of business deters the buyer from pushing too hard!

■ The total cost picture

All deals should aim to secure best value in total terms. This concept (sometimes referred to as 'Total Acquisition Cost' and 'Total Cost of Ownership') recognises that up-front price is only part of the total cost of the purchase. Other factors will contribute to the total initial cost being more than the unit price, and subsequent costs in terms of performance efficiency, maintenance, enhancements, etc. will add up to lifetime cost being greater than initial cost. In addition, comparison of different proposals from competing suppliers will involve distinguishing between 'hard money' components such as price, payment terms, etc. and 'soft money' factors which require value judgement, such as the quality of the product or service offered. Table 13.1 gives examples of price and non-price considerations.

The time-value of money is one non-price factor which can have a surprising impact on total cost. A prestige automobile manufacturer wished to invest in a new paint facility, and had received two similarly priced proposals from two (genuinely competing) suppliers. Based on price alone it was difficult to choose between them, but the payment phasing proposed by each supplier was different . . . one wanted a down

Table 13.1 Maximising value for money – some possible negotiating variables

Price	Maintenance	Length of contract
Discounts: Quantity	Spares	Terms and conditions
Preferred customer	Collection of rejects/surplus	Supply security
Price stability	Installation costs	Risk sharing
Price variation formula	Commissioning	Developments, enhancements
Price breakdown	Manuals, drawings, plans	Supplier relationship
Pricing policy	Parts book	Relationship with other suppliers
Payment terms	Tool kits	Exclusivity
Currency	Responsibilities	Confidentiality
Deferral of increases	Progress reports	Visits to supplier
Delivery costs	Consequential aspects	Visits to customers
Delivery dates	Training onsite/offsite	Visits to competitors
Delivery location(s)	Customisation: – Spec	Audit rights
Delivery frequency	– Printing	Third party liability
Insurance	– Finish	Favoured nations
Quality and specifications	Servicing	Sole supplier or not
Quality confidence (new supplier)	Health and safety	Liquidated damages
Performance guarantees	Product safety	'Guinea-pig' customer
Reliability	Packaging	Product endorsement
Free samples	Returnable packaging	International contracts
Assistance with promotions/trials	Materials for testing	Who completes the paperwork
Flexibility to changes	Translations	Guarding/security
Consignment stock	Consolidated stock	Buffer stops
Emergency response	Buy-back agreement	
Inclusion of other requirements	Lead time/availability	

payment 'up front' which was higher than the other, but the second payment was asked for at a later date and the final instalment was less. Evaluation of each total cost in present-value terms opened up a clear distinction between the two similarly priced proposals and showed which supplier to go with, all other factors being equal.

The price and non-price items listed in table 13.1 are sometimes illustrated in the form of an iceberg: the price can be seen sticking out of the water, but it is riding on a vast number of less visible non-price factors (see figure 5.1, chapter 5). If the buyer aims only to reduce price, it not only attacks the supplier's profitability, but the reduction potential is limited only to the eighth (in iceberg terms) of what might be achieved if instead the focus is on the *total* cost. It is far more productive to attack the cost base. Depending on circumstances, this may be done by building up one's own cost picture and then challenging the supplier's position, or the search for significant cost reduc-tion may be a collaborative buyer–seller activity.

Searching for best-value deals therefore requires buyers not just to judge the total worth of a supplier's offer, but also to evaluate the optimum way of approaching suppliers for proposals in the first place. In some cases this may mean seeking offers from two or more suppliers whilst in others the buyer may deem it better to approach just one. This exposes the difference between the cost of the purchase (price and non-price factors) and the cost of purchasing, i.e. the operational costs incurred in the acquisition process. When the former is small then the cost of the search for best price, etc. is proportionally large – the effort may indeed deliver savings but these are insufficient to reward the cost of it.

Getting round behind price

A supplier makes a price proposal, the buyer says 'how do you arrive at that figure?' The seller, ready for just that question, launches into the process of justifying the price position. Another supplier asks for a price increase, the buyer asks 'why?' Again the seller is prepared . . . and in both the cases the buyer is trapped in what might be termed the 'logic tunnel'. Challenging prices 'head on' like this is not often productive, not just because the supplier is prepared but because the supporting logic may not be the whole story. It satisfactorily explains what is being asked for but in reality is merely a plausible 'cover story' for another reason behind the pricing basis which may not be acceptable for public airing. So the aim is to get round the back of the supplier's thinking on price, not to challenge it at face value in a 'convince me' showdown. Figure 13.1 illustrates this and is explained in more detail.

Pricing policy and its objective

Pricing policies are the various ways in which price can be used to achieve certain objectives. Some examples are:

- *Cost-plus* pricing: to cover costs and to make the required profit on top
- *Marginal cost* pricing: prices are sufficient to pay the incremental costs of providing the product or service and to make a profit contribution. These are the variable costs which depend on volume, fixed costs having already been allocated. Marginal costs are thus lower than cost-plus and may be used by the supplier to win new business, or to fill a final increment of production capacity in a most profitable way.
- Pricing *to meet or to beat competition*
- *Penetration pricing:* to capture business or market share currently in the hands of the competition
- *Skimming* pricing, or *premium* pricing: to obtain an additional premium on top of normal profit, knowing that customers will still pay because the item is prestigious, in short supply, available from only one source, etc.

Company profitability and financial status

Under normal circumstances a supplier's pricing policy may be steady (e.g. in the sense that it governs the pricing for all products over a long period) or may be designed

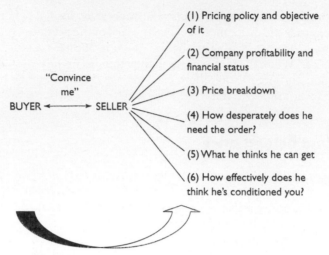

Figure 13.1 What is there 'round the back of the supplier'?

to achieve a specific short-term goal for one product (e.g. market penetration). Both approaches assume that the company is in control of its own destiny.

But what if the company is fearful of impending bankruptcy and is more concerned with cash flow than profit? Another company may face the need to reverse a deteriorating performance in order to maintain shareholders' confidence and to prevent adverse comment from city analysts. Such pressures may dictate that salespeople go for high prices and/or high increases, which will doubtless be justified by 'understandable' reasons such as currency fluctuations or movement in raw material prices. The buyer may end up accepting all or part of the logic – and paying up. However a better solution for both parties may well be to keep prices low but to shorten payment terms (to help cash flow) or to set up a longer contract (to demonstrate confidence in the company). Such avenues will not be open to the buyer who has not researched what is really driving the supplier to take a particular stance on price at the time in question.

Price breakdown

This is about understanding the logical basis for the supplier's price or requested increase. However, understanding does *not* mean acceptance of what is requested. Assuming that there will be a negotiation with the supplier, then the value of analysing the price breakdown is that it increases buyer confidence (through feeling prepared) and may identify flaws in the supplier's logic, thus giving the buyer a negotiating advantage to push for the price they need rather than that the supplier wants.

With a new supplier, the value of Purchasing Price and Cost Analysis is that it also indicates whether or not the supplier may have made errors in pricing, or whether the prices are pitched too low such that, although the supplier wins the order, the revenue earned fails to support the operation, forcing them eventually to come back for a price increase.

How desperately does the seller need your order?

In many ways here is a parallel to what was said about company profitability and financial status. But this time the focus is the supplier's representative: a salesperson who has hopes, fears, a mortgage and other financial liabilities,interests outside work, family matters, and so on. Just how much do buyers know about their sales counterparts? The answer usually is very little. If this is so then there is a rich vein of information to be explored which is directly relevant to that salesperson's thinking about you and the prices asked.

For example, what does the buyer know about the salesperson's targets:

■ what are they?
■ are they set on an annual or quarterly basis?
■ is the end of the target period now due? – and how are they doing?
■ is yours the final order which will bring them up to their boss's expectations?
■ if so, how much might they concede to ensure they win the order?

Many other facets of the relationship between them and you are relevant. If they do not already supply you, are there reasons (aside from the increased business) which would make them try hard to supply on your terms? For example, perhaps yours is a prestigious company which they need to be seen supplying to. Perhaps you are expanding in a market area (sector or geography) where they also wish to expand.

It may be even simpler. The salesperson goes on holiday tonight and needs one more order to stay on target. If *you* don't give it they will have to start over again with another potential customer, if they can still get in to see their buyer in what remains of the day. Perhaps it would be better to make a final concession to you and then it is in the bag.

These are some of the influences and pressures on the seller as they think about you and your price. Only one glimpse into their thinking is needed for the buyer to realise that a firm price, apparently built on a solid bedrock of closely reasoned logic, is in fact far more fluid and subjective than is made out to be the case. The message for the buyer is: be clear about what price you feel is right and, assuming that it is lower than what is being asked, go for it.

What do they think they can get?

This is all about image: how you and your company appear to the supplier. Do you look like an 'easy touch' with a track record of paying the asking price, or the increase, with only a token challenge? Or do you look mean, lean and likely to give the salesperson a hard time (assuming, that is, that they bother to stay around for such treatment and do not head off for an easier prospect elsewhere). Who knocked on whose door? Did you ask the salesperson to come in, perhaps unwittingly giving the impression that you had a problem with your existing source? Or did they make the contact, seemingly eager to get your business?

These issues relate to the image presented to the supply market by you, your colleagues and your company. Realising this, forward-looking procurement teams are deciding positively how they want to be seen and are managing their impact, rather than letting image look after itself.

Image is transmitted to suppliers through the behaviour and appearance of buyers and their surroundings: by the documents they issue (enquiry letters, bidding formalities, information brochures, things said in passing to suppliers by non-buyer people in your company). It also depends on the type of business you are in and whether it is a private firm or government department. In some cases, image can be the deciding factor in the salesperson's mind when setting a price for you, shaded up or down by what they have quoted to other customers and got away with there.

How effectively have they 'conditioned' you to agree with what they want?

Often unknown to buyers, sellers take systematic actions to 'condition' buyers' behaviour. Such actions are not confined to buying and selling. Indeed the concept originated with the Russian physiologist I. V. Pavlov (1849–1936) , well known for his experimental work on animal behaviour and particularly to do with 'conditioned reflexes'.

In the procurement context, 'conditioning' means 'creating an expectation in the mind of the buyer which leads to an appropriate response desired by the seller', e.g. the acceptance of an adequate but worthwhile price increase as a result of repeated suggestions to the buyer that a much larger increase could be on the way.

Sellers are trained to 'condition' the behaviour of buyers so that they will react in a predictable way which is favourable to the seller. Most people in the customer company are unaware of this subtle process, and certainly only a few have developed techniques to counteract and reverse it. For example, what is a buyer's normal reaction when the supplier advises that a price increase is imminent? Many fire off an order to get in ahead of the price increase – which is exactly what the salesperson wants. Similarly, a supplier telephones the buyer two or three times to signal that a possible 9 per cent price increase is in the pipeline, and then writes to request only a 5 per cent increase. 'As a result of our conversations', the seller says, 'I have been able to reduce the increase from 9 to 5 per cent', etc. The 5 per cent raise will probably be accepted without argument because the buyer is relieved it is not as bad as expected.

And many who are on the receiving end of this technique fail to learn from the experience. One real-life example saw conditioning being used simultaneously by a supplier on customers across a number of countries to win successfully a 15 per cent price increase. The following year, a 5.7 per cent increase was needed and so the sellers started the conditioning process again with phone calls to the buyers talking about a 'significant increase' to come. One buyer's reaction: 'Look, after last year's price rise there's no way I can accept a double-digit increase this year.' 'That's OK', replied the seller, 'I'll hold it down to 8.9 per cent for you!' Another customer feeling that they had satisfactorily asserted themselves, but at the expense of the bottom line – and they never knew it.

There is more to a deal than deciding that you want it – psychology plays a key part.

Conditioning works because it prepares the recipient's mind for a certain outcome, then achieves acceptance because the actual outcome is not as bad as expected. It works because many unaware customers concentrate too much on the 'content' or specification aspect of a deal and assume that once this is settled then the rest (e.g. commercial factors) follows automatically. They ignore the impact of 'how' the deal is arrived at . . . the 'process'.

So, supply chain costs are vulnerable to being increased by the conditioning process. Analytical efforts to reduce supply chain waste can themselves be wasted by planting ideas in the buyer's mind. Price increases can be eased through, and the effects of post-contract specification changes can be used to lever high added costs into the deal. We are also conditioned to believe that, inflation being what it is, costs will increase as time passes. Some even talk of price 'escalation' formulae! Such reflex thinking ignores the huge cost-reduction impact that can come from new technology and better ways of working.

The best protection to being conditioned is simply to be aware that the process exists and 'might be being done to you'. Get into the habit of self-questioning 'am I being conditioned?' whenever the supplier makes suggestions which will erode the quality of the deal which you have worked so hard to create. Strive to 'keep the seller selling' both before and after the contract is made. In this mode the seller is working hard to win the buyer's interest and will keep improving the deal with this aim in mind. What stops them are well-intentioned phrases such as 'your quality is excellent: no one else can touch it!'

But still further steps can be taken to keep the seller selling because they are uncertain of the buyer's intentions. Now it is the buyer's turn to be pro-active in channelling the seller's thinking. For example:

- do not always declare the full volume required in a price enquiry
- time the purchase to coincide with 'sensitive' times of the supplier's year (i.e. towards their financial year end, or at the end of seller's target period.)
- use open questions to get the seller talking and uncertain of your precise intentions. They tend to say more under these conditions
- prepare the supplier's mind with information about your intended cost-reduction plans; invite them to meet to discuss price decreases for the next period of the contract. Do not call them in to receive their advice about next year's prices.
- release data about published downward price-trends of supplier's raw materials
- use their price-lists as a basis for challenging how they arrive at price and to identify logic-flaws. Do not accept them as a *fait-accompli*. Seek to expose flaws in their logic or the data used to justify the price levels

'Getting round behind price': Summary

Buyers are often made to feel that price is unshakeable and established by impeccable logic which cannot be argued with. The facts are quite different and, as well as the logic, there are many subjective factors crossing the seller's mind when they are setting a price – for you – at this time.

> Prices are made to look like they have been worked out. The reality is that they are 'made up'.

Because the process is subjective, buyers should feel that their own view about 'what is reasonable' is just as valid as the supplier's view – only more so since you are the one who is going to pay. Be cautious though that understanding how price is arrived at does not automatically lead to you accepting it. Just because you can see how the numbers are arrived at does not mean that you have to agree with the answer. What's asked may exceed the money in your budget. 'I understand your reasoning but cannot afford it' is often the best answer to flawless logic.

How the buyer takes the debate with the seller is the next issue

■ How best to improve a price proposal

Since prices are 'evolved from subjective judgements and not fixed solely by calculations', it will pay to put pressure on them. But have you also considered that pushing too hard to lower the price, or not pushing at all, might make the total costs go *up*? The reason is that final prices actually agreed between buyers and sellers, which might indeed have their origins in a cost-plus calculation, are ultimately 'made in the head'. Pushing for reductions in an aggressive way conditions the seller to want to get their own back – by charging high for everything that is extra, or coming in with claims. Price itself goes down, but total costs increase. Not pushing at all, or doing it in a weak way, conditions the seller to believe that 'money is not a problem' and that additions to the price will be accepted.

It is obvious that the buyer needs to find the right balance between pushing too hard and pushing too little. On this balance lies the optimum price, sitting on what we can call the 'Price Plateau'. Let's examine the concept in more detail.

They say 'you get what you pay for', but there comes a point of diminishing returns where the incremental extra benefits do not justify the extra costs. Imagine that you are contracting in some musical entertainment to accompany a major public relations event at your company. There are at least three possibilities. One is to engage a local amateur – cheap, yes, but possibly embarrassing if they have neither the charisma nor the experience to handle such an occasion. People will remember the PR event as being a disaster.

What about hiring a megastar? No problem with the entertainment's quality – but was it really right to spend *so* much money on it, given that a singer can only sing so many songs in the allotted time, and anyway the event was not intended to be a concert. In-between lies the right choice: someone who is not so well known, or maybe unknown, but who does an excellent job and for less money. Participants feel well entertained and, more important, feel that what was provided was absolutely in tune with the intention to provide an effective high-quality PR event.

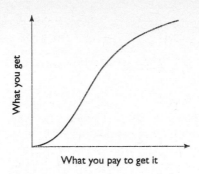

Figure 13.2 The price plateau (1)

Figure 13.2 plots 'what you get' versus 'what you pay to get it'. Since our assessment of 'what we get', and our satisfaction with it, is subjective the graph is qualitative, but still relevant. As we begin to pay more than rock-bottom price we get demonstrable increase in benefits. Then there is an optimum, above which no matter how much we pay there is a limit to what extra can be provided. Another way of demonstrating this is with car prices. The difference in what you get (capability, performance, prestige, etc.) between a low-price standard family saloon and a bottom-of-the-range luxury car will be considerable. But does the extra benefit offered by the top model in the same luxury car range (compared with the standard model with fewer extras) really represent a similar proportional increase in value-for-money compared with that gained by going from family saloon to luxury car? The answer is subject to criteria built into each person's own value system . . . but the shape of the S-curve is what is relevant rather than its position versus figure 13.2's vertical axis.

Each point on the S-curve signifies value for money (VFM), so let us now plot VFM against price. This is figure 13.3. The price at the plateau represents optimum value-for-money. Suppose this is the price actually offered by the supplier, and now you want to put pressure on it. What happens now depends critically on *how* you do it. The balance point will shift in one of four directions into the sectors superimposed on the price plateau. The horizontal line of the 'crosswires' is about rapport and *feelings* – below is 'cold', above is 'warm'. The vertical line represents the *challenge* offered by the buyer – left is 'tough', right is 'easy'. Examining the four different buyer styles reveals the following when used in the price-challenge context:

COLD–TOUGH A style favoured by the traditional macho buyer. It is recognised by power-plays such as: 'Your price is uncompetitive, you'll have to cut it if you want the business.' Alternatively the buyer seeks cost-cutting measures: 'We don't want to pay that much so we'll do this part of the job ourselves'; or 'OK, you might normally use five people on these contracts but we're telling you to do it with three.'

How does this make the seller feel? At best, they will go along with it but hold the buyer responsible if things go wrong. At worst, the mental set is 'OK, but I'll get my own back.' Value-for-money is sub-optimal.

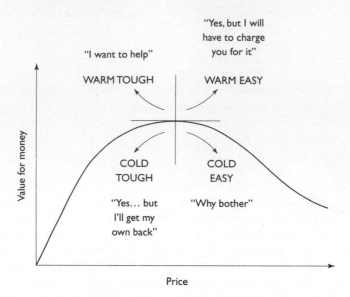

Figure 13.3 The price plateau (2)

COLD–EASY The buyer is not really bothering. In the context of, say, the price being affected by a delivery problem or a quality reject, the position taken is 'Everyone makes mistakes, how much is the extra charge?' There is no attempt to get to grips with the problem or to motivate the supplier's interest in solving or minimising it. It leaves the seller thinking 'Why bother to get it right in the first place?' Again, the casualty is value-for-money, and ultimately the fortunes of the buyer's company.

WARM–EASY Things are now improving in that the buyer *is* making efforts to improve matters and to enlist the seller's collaboration in the process. But underlying this is an acceptance that nothing comes for free. 'We have a problem here' says the buyer, 'and we need your good ideas to solve it. But of course we'll pay.' Or, 'so long as quality and service are OK then price is a secondary consideration'. And a favourite from specialists who are not acquainted with the commercial sensitivity of what they say: 'Your product is excellent – you are the only people who can meet our needs.' With dollar signs swimming in front of the seller's eyes the mental set is: 'Yes, of course we can help, but we will have to charge extra.' More value might be obtained, but at a price higher than necessary.

WARM–TOUGH This is the *essential* buyer style when the item or service acquired is critical to the business and the buyer needs the seller perhaps more than the seller needs the sale. Buyers now switch on the charm *and* the challenge. 'We're really excited about this new opportunity – we need your help so that we can both benefit.

What can you do to help us reduce the prices?' And, if it is genuine, 'if we are successful then you'll be successful'. But it takes much more than glib words. The buyer's whole attitude must reflect regard for the seller as a professional equal, as an interesting individual and as a creative partner in a problem-solving process. The buyer is successful in exciting the seller to reach for targets which the seller may think are not possible, but the seller *is* going to try because not to do so would be to let the buyer down and disappoint them. The seller's mental set is 'I want to help', a decision which has been made voluntarily and not as a result of buyer-bullying. Value-for-money soars, becoming infinitely high when the supply is offered for free! And that *can* and *does* happen if the seller wants it to.

The message in all of this is 'Don't limit your targets and price challenge to what the facts can justify: feed off feelings and motivate the seller's to work for you.' Whilst it might be difficult to put figures on a concept like 'value' and to calculate where the price plateau is, there is no doubt about the feelings that can be created in sellers' minds as a result of buyer tactics used on them.

Heads down and immersed in cost-plus price data and technical considerations, the many people in a company whose work impacts on the procurement process (i.e. *not* just the buyers) are often blissfully unaware of the impact of their behaviour on the seller's attitude to the business. Best of breed buyers are highly aware of price *and* psychology. And whilst they may not know exactly where the price plateau *is*, they soon know when they move off it – and make sure that movement is into 'wanting to help' territory.

■ Managing price 'in future'

Whilst there are several ways to keep price under control 'in future' within the framework of a six months or longer-term contract, some work better for the buyer than others. Figure 13.4 illustrates. All methods have their place and it is up to the buyer to select the best fit in any given circumstances.

Fixed prices for the term of the contract are good if there is real certainty that market prices will increase during the contract period. However this is a guess which both the supplier and the buyer will be making and the former may well include a contingency for the price rises which might come along. The buyer's sense of security that price increases have been avoided may thus be false since an increment of 'possible price increase' is in fact already being paid from the outset. If the supplier's own purchase prices fall, or if innovations create cost reductions for them, the buyer feels none of the benefit.

One way of protecting both parties is to rely on price variation formulae (PVA). Here the total price is represented in terms of its component parts (e.g. materials, labour and overheads) and the initial value of each is pegged to an index which may change in future as a result of inflation effects, new technology, etc. This mathematical approach may be appropriate if the initial pricing policy is a cost-plus one. However if this is not

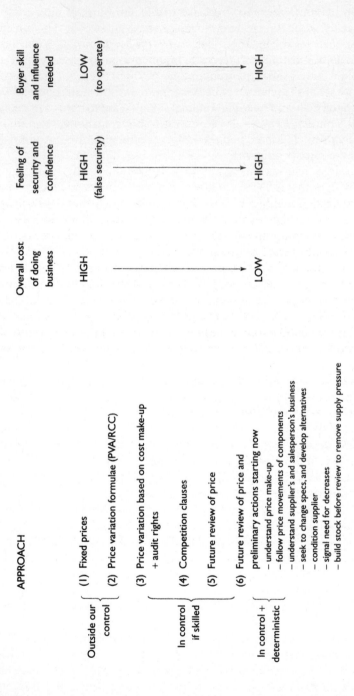

Figure 13.4 How best to control in future?

so (e.g. the supplier may have won the deal on the basis of a premium pricing policy) then prices for the life of the contract will be higher than would be the case if based at the outset on actual costs of supply or competitive market pricing. General experience also indicates that the formula is more often triggered by the seller seeking a price increase than by a buyer seeking a reduction. The seller tends to be more in control. This is because they see the whole picture (i.e. general market price trends and indexed indicators *plus* their own purchase and internal costs) whereas the buyer tends only to see the external numbers. Not surprising then that one customer company has become so conditioned to seeing prices rising over time that they refer to the 'controlling' mechanism not as a PVA but as an RCC – a rising cost contingency!

An insight to supplier costs can be gained by negotiating audit rights at the outset. This can be helpful but care has to be taken in terms of managing the relationship – hence a higher level of buyer skill being needed compared with the previous approaches. One adverse consequence may be that an atmosphere of mistrust builds up as the seller is continually required to prove effectively that they have been honest in their calculations. Neither should we lose sight of the fact that the time spent on proving that the calculations are right may better be spent in searching jointly for a cost reduction. An extension of the audit approach is to insert a competition clause into the contract whereby the supplier commits to sell to you at the same price as he does to an equivalent other customer. The challenge here is to police it.

Finally we have two bolder approaches – bolder in that they do not seek to pin down the supplier at the outset but rely more on the buyer's ability to negotiate a price review in future. The success of this will be limited if action is left until the review time arrives. Better to start preparing the ground now by building knowledge about the supplier's price make-up (information is often more freely available in the relaxed atmosphere of post-contract euphoria than during the negotiations themselves) and to start conditioning them to the fact that cost-reduction efforts will be sought constantly during the course of the contract.

Chapter fourteen

Keeping costs out of supply chains . . . by ironing out market distortions

The popular view of the supply market is too simplistic in that it is believed to be genuinely competitive, i.e. competitive forces always drive the best deal towards the buyer who simply has to compare offers and, after some ritualistic browbeating to improve them, accepts the best.

Genuine competition does of course exist in many cases but even then the customer company's actions can negate this favourable situation and allow higher costs into the supply chain. This is discussed in more detail later. But let us assume that the buying company has got it right: a needs-oriented specification, no buying signals leaked out unwittingly to the supplier, flexible purchase tactics, and an objective analysis of where the competitive advantage lies between buyer and seller. However another challenge presents itself in the form of a distorted market, i.e. an absence of competitive forces favouring the buyer. Most commonly this shows up as a monopoly; less obviously, as a cartel. Either way, if the buyer cannot deal effectively with these situations, supply chain costs take quantum leaps upwards of more than 30–50 per cent can be expected.

■ Why monopolies? . . . and what to do?

A monopoly exists when there is only one supplier who can provide the particular product or service needed. Why does this happen? Here are some reasons:

- the supplier has a specific capability or a strong 'proprietary item' position which prevents others producing similar products
- the source may be specified by an inflexible end-user, leaving the buyer no flexibility to look for alternatives, be they new sources or a standard, rather than unique, specification
- the buyer may be 'locked in' to a situation which makes it totally uneconomic to re-source. One example might be a computer system where, to deviate from the chosen system and vendor, may lead to hardware and software incompatibilities
- government policy or political considerations may require buyers to use a local source, or may indicate that some others are undesirable for whatever reason

■ corporate rules may direct that purchases should be made from manufacturing units within the same group

The monopoly may therefore be real (i.e. externally imposed) or self-inflicted. Either way the buyer perceives that their freedom of action is restricted and tends to feel 'beaten before they start!' But the idea behind the above list is to show that the time taken to understand why the monopoly situation exists may well reveal a hitherto untried course of action which will solve the problem. The aim is to create room for manoeuvre and/or to identify areas where the buyer has some power over the seller. To assist this, where the monopoly is genuinely externally generated, here is a menu of possible actions to take:

■ source worldwide
■ avoid price as the main focus and instead work on the total cost of doing business by considering non-price issues such as delivery, packaging, payment terms, storage, after-sales service, etc. All of these contribute to total costs, but are 'less visible' issues and provide an opportunity to negotiate savings even though the supplier stands firm on price
■ seek to improve value for money by getting additional services included 'free' in the price
■ develop another supplier locally
■ increase supplier dependency by placing more business with them, thereby increasing their reliance on your custom
■ look for a 'corporate soft spot' that can be challenged (e.g. most monopoly suppliers do not like it to be seen that they are exploiting their position of strength)
■ join forces with other companies (who may not necessarily be your competitors) taking the same supplies, thereby increasing the dependency of the supplier 'on the group'.
■ separate the business and personal components in the deal. Deals are done between people, not companies. Encourage the seller to come over as 'the friend who wants to help' rather than as an 'anonymous' company sales representative. Engage their creativity in finding out ways in which they want to help reduce supply costs.
■ consider making a 'one-time buy' to meet current and future needs, thereby eliminating the effect of big 'take it or leave it' price increases in future

■ Why cartels? . . . and what to do?

A cartel is a group of suppliers who act in an organised fashion amongst themselves. They decide which of them should be allowed to present the most attractive bid in response to a potential customer's invitation to make an offer. The 'successful supplier' will be allowed to submit his price proposal whilst the other 'competitors' will make higher and therefore unattractive offers, often called 'cover prices'. Cartels are clearly undesirable from a number of viewpoints but, whilst not excusing them, it has to be said that cartel behaviour can be triggered by aggressive, closed behaviour on the part of buyers. There have been cases where suppliers, who genuinely wanted to collaborate with the potential customer, have been frightened off by macho and threatening buying tactics. The suppliers have then sought security by collaborating between themselves, with the bonus of higher profitability at the buyer's expense.

But how do buyers know when they are on the receiving end of cartel activity? The cartel tester, table 14.1, provides a first-level check which will either allay or raise buyer suspicion.

If a cartel is indicated, and because it has shown itself, then the buyer is forced into a reactive response with the chance of only limited success. For example it is often suggested that negotiating with the lowest bidder, having first built a stronger position by getting more data on cost breakdowns, etc., is appropriate. But the 'successful' supplier in a cartel situation is unlikely to yield, other than to make a cosmetic price adjustment, since they know they have already 'won' the business. If the purchase is significant enough to justify the effort, then it is usually necessary to cancel the whole bidding exercise and to start again. A successful and, this time, pro-active strategy, will be to approach the market in such a way as to make it difficult, if not impossible, for the cartel to operate. The new strategy and the buyer's approach will have the following characteristics:

- be unpredictable by not approaching the supply market in the same way time after time
- create uncertainty amongst the suppliers about certain aspects of the proposed deal (e.g. ask one supplier to quote unit rates, another to quote lump sum)
- disguise the fact that you are the customer by issuing bid invitations through a third party (e.g. a consultant engineer or a contractor who may be handling a number of different projects for different clients)
- introduce time pressure
- share the business rather than sole source it
- locate new suppliers outside the cartel

The key message is that buyer success depends on anticipating and then preventing cartels from operating, as opposed to using contingency plans after the cartel has been allowed to activate.

Table 14.1 The cartel tester

	Yes	No
Are all offered prices higher than expected?		
Are there patterns/trends as to who has won orders before?		
Are one or more suppliers reluctant to negotiate?		
Have one or more suppliers refused to bid?		
Are suppliers reluctant to enter into a long-term deal?		
Is the 'best price' significantly lower than the rest?		
Three or more 'yes' answers and a cartel may be operating		

■ But the true enemy is wasteful costs

The whole subject of monopolies and cartels introduces an adversarial tone into the debate about buyer–seller relationships at a time when the talk in business is about the opposite: partnerships, strategic alliances, outsourcing in order to rely more on supplier expertise, etc. However, it is true that customers will get the suppliers they deserve, and a procurement team (including the end-users) which creates self-inflicted monopolies, or triggers cartel behaviour, deserves to pay higher prices. Maybe even this is not a problem in those companies who enjoy huge profitability, for the time being. Companies who hurt themselves by macho approaches to the supply market usually exhibit adversarial behaviours both internally and externally. In purchasing inside these companies, 'strategy' is defined as 'a plan to defeat the enemy', and the enemy is seen to be the supplier.

But the really good companies are those who envision becoming better in every aspect of their operation. Suppliers are seen as an external resource that can contribute to success, although that philosophy does not stop the buyer from being streetwise and highly aware. Also, not all suppliers have the same importance and so relationships with them are carefully selected according to criticality. Therefore, for some purchases, the fact that relationships are cool and at arm's length doesn't really matter simply because the customer's business is not greatly dependent on that particular supply line. However, for key requirements, be they materials or services, the enemy is not the supplier, but 'waste' in the supply chain. This was covered in detail in chapter 5.

The better companies are successful at winning excellent and collaborative responses from key suppliers in attacking wasteful costs. Being seen as the customer who knows how to handle market distortions effectively is one way of looking professional to the seller, and gaining their respect and commitment to respond in a positive way to your needs. And recent case histories have shown that the prize is not just lower supply chain costs, but also competitive advantage for both the customer *and* the supplier.

Chapter fifteen

How suppliers can add value

To be in business and to concern oneself only with the internal workings of the firm is a very one-dimensional view of things and, ultimately, not viable. In looking up from the desk and out into the world, most companies then think of the customer as their *raison d'être*. But even this two-dimensional view is limited and ignores the input side of the trading equation. This is where the supply market is seen as a source of value, obtained at lowest total cost. Internal company activities then add intrinsic value to the raw materials or services acquired, and sales and marketing efforts create high perceived value in the mind of the customer, commensurate with the high price they are then willing to pay!

But even where the supply-side inputs to the business *are* acknowledged, procurement's priority tends to be set high or low by the amount of money being expended with suppliers. In reality it is better to view procurement's role by asking 'In what ways does the sustained success of our business depend on supply market behaviour?', rather than merely focussing on 'How much do we spend?' Proper regard for the 'third dimension', the supply side, can transform business results because suppliers are viewed in terms of what they might be able to contribute to the business, rather than as being a drain on hard-earned incoming revenue.

So, companies are increasingly depending on a high-quality supplier base to support their business goals. Partly this is due to the trend to contract-out more and more activity which previously was conducted in-house, enabling the company to focus more on doing what they do best, i.e. running the core business. The extent to which this is done is reflected in the percentage of total incoming sales revenue which is spent on the purchases of materials and services. Although this has typically run at around 55 per cent in a manufacturing company it is now becoming more common to find figures up at 70–80 per cent. With this high dependency on external suppliers, tomorrow's challenge for procurement managers effectively becomes:

> to manage a large part of our company which we do not own; which we cannot see; and which is staffed by people who we do not employ

Couple the above trend with the strategy of many companies to reduce the size of their supplier base, and the dependence on external sources becomes very great indeed. So, with companies deliberately putting more eggs into fewer baskets who is making sure that the 'baskets' are up to the job?

■ Sizing up supplier relationships

What is required is more than traditional supplier appraisal. Time was when financial checks on the supplier were the main focus of such pre-contract checks. Now, as production tolerances tighten and quality control regimes challenge waste, the supplier's ability to assure product or service quality is paramount. But if suppliers are increasingly to be regarded as an 'offsite' part of our company then they need to think like us as well as act in the way we strive to. Companies who have the vision of becoming 'best' in the foreseeable future need 'best' supply partners in that venture. The pressure to develop such relationships is such that some large companies are assigning a senior manager on a full-time basis to establish a comprehensive supplier management programme. But it is all too easy for these programmes to give too much attention to establishing criteria against which supplier partners may be selected, and too little to how the relationships should be managed and measured. The programmes end up looking like traditional, albeit updated, supplier appraisal systems.

The breakthrough comes when we stop sizing up suppliers at arm's length, telling them that they have to improve and then leaving them to it. The thinking and planning power of many 'customer' companies often exceeds that of the smaller suppliers who cannot get started on the road to performance improvement simply because they do not know where best to start. And often the improvement step needed is so great that it looks impossible – and *is*, if attempted in one go. If a major change is broken down into smaller steps, then each step looks achievable. This is the basis of the 'Ten(d) to Zero' (Smithard) programme for improving supplier performance. Each of several (typically 8–12) aspects of supplier performance are defined in ten degrees of attainment: '10' defines how we would recognise a poorest performance, '0' defines the best and other numbers the shades between. The aim is to 'tend' towards best performance in all areas. This is achieved by regular monitoring and then feedback of results to the supplier concerned. And it works.

In the words of a supplier's sales director:

> When our customer came to us with this idea, it was the last thing we wanted to do on top of all our other problems. All I can say now is how glad I am that we went along with it. We are not only pleasing that customer with a vastly improved performance, but we are more competitive overall and winning more orders. **Win–win**!

However, the hallmark of a quality supplier-relationship programme is that it focusses on the future as well as the present, and success as well as failure. The 'Affirmative Vendor Improvement Programme' (AVIP) (Russill, 1992) does this, being based on the acceptance of the supplier as a very important part of our business. It is the supplier's attitude to business and to its continual improvement that is the key. If the buyer is prepared to invest time and creativity in putting a supplier on the improvement path, then the reward is to be seen as a preferred customer. This does *not* mean solving the supplier's problems for them, but instead working with them to develop their own problem-solving capability and then motivating them to apply these skills. A good model to work to is the well-researched 'Characteristics of High-Performing Organisations'.

Elements of an affirmative vendor improvement programme

Select suppliers: position the relationship; what are we buying?

Open communication channels . . . even when there is not a problem

Understand supplier's business strategy and objectives

Be more visible: publicise plans, brochures, supplier conferences

Market yourself as a preferred customer: procurement marketing

Implement strategic supplier plans: provide improvement framework;
place buyer at supplier's site; create continuous improvement capability

---

Characteristics of high-performing, spirited organisations

clearly stated vision and purpose
strong collective alignment with that vision and purpose
culture and organisation shaped to support purpose
authority delegated as low as possible
a lean and simple structure
hierarchy kept to a minimum
dedication to the professional growth of employees
people treated as professionals: empowered, trusted, competent
support for innovation and ideas for change
toleration (but not duplication) of mistakes
teamwork instead of in-fighting
high emphasis on ethics and integrity

(James A. Ritscher Associates, 1983, 1060 Beacon Street, Brookline, MA 02146, USA)

The organisation referred to may be a football team, a symphony orchestra, or indeed a supplier. Research shows that consistently successful organisations, regardless of their role, exhibit these same characteristics. They make an excellent profile against which to measure supplier performance because it becomes a set of attributes as much about attitude as about functional excellence. Share with such suppliers the purpose of your business and the part they play in it, and motivate them with your vision of what can be achieved together in future. This is the driver for continual improvement, whilst Ten(d) to Zero and AVIP techniques are the vehicles for getting there.

> If suppliers are to be regarded as part of our company, it makes sense to measure them by the same standards that we use for ourselves.

■ Eliminating wasteful costs . . . by joint problem-solving with motivated suppliers

Where there's a will there's a way. And it is only those customer companies who motivate suppliers to collaborate on finding ways of removing supply-chain costs who win the big benefits. These are the companies who really 'breakthrough' into realising quantum-leap improvements in their supply arrangements such that not only significant cost reductions are achieved, but also gains in competitive advantage.

Lesser companies try to work out solutions by themselves and then impose them on suppliers, a one-sided approach that only delivers a fraction of the benefits, and then only temporarily. But why do they do this? Part of the answer lies in the customer attitude to their supplier. Many customer companies have the mental set that says 'we know best' and, in prescribing solutions to suppliers, fail to tap into the supplier's own expertise and creativity. Then again, many do not trust their suppliers and fall into the trap of thinking that a more open and collaborative relationship with them will make them vulnerable to being exploited since, they feel, the supplier will be in a stronger position. Being realistic, this can and does happen: but not with suppliers who have been chosen carefully and who have both the capability *and* an empathy with the customer company. Empathy does not just mean 'similar interests' but also implies that the supplier has the same values as regards the integrity of their business dealings, plus a belief that it is better to forget short-term exploitation of customers in the interests of achieving mutual benefits in the longer term.

Whether we like it or not, the twin demands of being able to meet ever-changing customer requirements *and* to keep up with the accelerating pace of technological change, whilst also remaining successful as a business, inevitably requires a rethink at the input end of the business. But not for everything we buy. It depends on the criticality and strategic importance of the products or services acquired, and the Supply Positioning technique can distinguish the 'strategic few' close relationships required from the 'tactical many' arm's-length transactions. Let us be clear though that 'close' relationships do not mean blind trust and long-term commitments to buy. In simple terms it means teamwork between people who get on well together, who respect each others' companies, and who share a view that together they can achieve a 'breakthrough' which neither can achieve on their own. It is also better to look at things on a 'project-by-project' basis rather than to assume that, having decided to let the supplier into our thinking, then we have to stay like that for ever more. There *will* always be a relationship, but let us put it that 'friendship' will always be there whilst full-time collaboration need only be commissioned when appropriate to do so. Technologies change, your needs as a customer change, new suppliers emerge . . . and the buyer needs the flexibility to change sourcing strategies as demands dictate.

How to motivate suppliers

So what can be done to motivate the supplier to help achieve breakthrough? Motivational theory shows that all the inspiring leadership in the world is ineffective if the recipient of it is consumed with concerns and uncertainties which haunt every waking thought. These are termed 'demotivators'. Figure 15.1 introduces the 'big M' – a complete model for motivating people whether they be people who work in our company or in the supplier's. Before positive motivators have a chance of working, demotivators have to be removed or significantly reduced. Unfortunately many

Demotivators are holding us back

Figure 15.1 Motivating supplier performance (1)

customer companies are much better at demotivating suppliers than inspiring them.
Examples of demotivators are:

- late payment or supplier cash-flow problems
- being a difficult or inflexible customer
- being a 'poor image' customer
- antagonism
- unrealistic requirements, many changes
- making a salesperson look bad
- too many requests for quotes, but no business
- feeling played off against other suppliers
- trust/confidences breached
- perception of being discriminated against
- feeling 'screwed down' or insufficiently rewarded
- contract obligations not honoured
- no feedback or praise
- personal incompatibility
- lack of respect
- fear of failure
- unclear targets
- interference/time consumed thoughtlessly

Once demotivators have been tidied up, then two complementary mindsets have to be
implanted in the supplier: 'I'm *expected* to perform well', and 'I *want* to perform well'
(figure 15.2). The following lists some of the practical actions which create the
'*expected*' response:

- high-class 'in control' procurement process and systems
- clear, precise, performance-oriented specifications
- effective communication channels
- 'I know who I should talk to'
- contract exists
- compliance is expected with what both parties perceive to be a fair contract
- performance is measured with feedback
- evidence of integrated team effort by customer

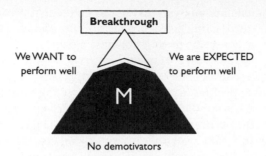

We WANT to perform well

We are EXPECTED to perform well

No demotivators

Figure 15.2 Motivating supplier performance (2)

What can be done in addition to make the supplier 'WANT' to perform well? Examples are:

■ fair, ethical treatment
■ shared objectives and involvement in setting them
■ collaboration to realise them
■ exciting vision and strategic 'fit' between supplier and customer
■ a contractual horizon exists which means that the supplier need not fear losing the business in the short to medium term
■ two-way performance measurement
■ professional treatment
■ contact maintained even when there is no contract
■ supplier feels rewarded and not exploited, and personally feels 'obliged'
■ capability recognised and respected
■ freedom to act and innovate
■ empathy
■ opportunity for more business
■ supplier is 'sold' on the total benefits of supplying the customer (Procurement Marketing)
■ win/'perceived win'
■ praise/publicity for a job well done

Experience shows that when the three sides of the triangle are in place potential breakthrough becomes reality. Real examples include a dramatic elimination of stock levels from three months' worth to 30 minutes (think of the finance saving); a reduction in project time from 90 days to 15 (think of the extra revenue from better asset utilisation); 30 per cent cost savings by bringing in a new supplier to combat a monopoly supply situation (but think also of the reduced risk versus previously being exposed to just one key source).

Areas for the joint attack on wasteful costs

So, with a motivated supplier on board, on what issues should joint problem solving be focussed? Four areas hold the answers:

- **do an 'ABC' customer analysis** in order to find which particular supply chains (in which you are the link between your supplier and your customer) represent the biggest cost and value to your business. Focus on these
- **reveal the existing cost elements** in the supply chain (e.g. supplier manufacturing costs, delivery costs, inventory costs, etc.)
- **assess cost-time profiles** (e.g. where is there waiting time; at what stages in the manufacturing and supply process are the biggest cost elements incurred, etc.)
- **define the actual process** whereby a customer 'need' transmits back up the supply chain to create a supplier response, and also define the ideal process. Then look for differences between actual and ideal, and work to close the gaps.

A project-by-project approach is advocated and this implies that close collaboration is needed only for a finite time. That might be the case if a major breakthrough is sought, but good companies are usually not happy about resting on the new status quo, regardless of how good it is. Continual improvement is expected and indeed is necessary if 'best' companies are to stay that way. Equally, a customer company is unlikely to move from supplier to supplier once a high-performing supply chain has been established. A longer-term operational relationship makes sense, subject to satisfactory performance continuing on *both* sides of the supplier–customer relationship. It is at this stage that the methodology of running and improving the supply chain must be supplemented by the business management skills needed to ensure that the source of supply remains viable and committed. More about this later in 'Key Supplier Account Management'.

Deciding who to work with

If close collaboration with a supplier is seen as the key to achieving a supply chain breakthrough, then 'supplier appraisal' takes on a new dimension. Careful assessment needs to get well under the skin of the potential partner. Here are some of the supplier assessment criteria used by three multi-national companies – 'A, B and C' – operating in different business sectors:

Company A	Company B	Company C
Capability	Business capability	Vision
Capacity	Availability of products	Commitment
Cost/technology advantage	or services	Capability:
Continuous improvement?	Avoidance of conflicts	– planning
Competitive edge	of interests	– diagnosing
– lowest overall cost	Financial position	– decision making
– world-class performance	Quality assurance systems	– implementation
potential	Management structure and	– evaluation
Trust	company culture	Behaviour

All show a far deeper approach than is traditionally used for 'supplier appraisal', and Company C's evaluation is particularly interesting in view of its emphasis on 'soft' or qualitative issues like 'behaviour'. Nevertheless some 41 detailed measures are in place covering all their headings from vision to behaviour, 20 being allocated in the latter category alone. Also relevant is this company's emphasis on the overall 'process' capability of the supplier. The inference is that if these scores are acceptable then, as a 'natural' consequence, the supply company will be doing well in terms of results areas such as 'lowest overall cost' and 'financial position'.

The object of all this, in the words of one of these companies, is 'to differentiate, develop and retain highly competitive external suppliers with whom mutually beneficial business relationships are developed, providing maximum added value that contributes to our business objectives'. Whilst highly structured evaluation processes are useful in focussing the mind, for making comparisons and for explaining decisions afterwards, a danger is to overlook the human angle and the value of intuition. Real breakthroughs come as a result of a meeting of minds rather than a mechanistic meeting of acceptance criteria. This is reflected in the thinking of some other companies who feel, rather than calculate, their way into a close relationship. Acceptability criteria *can* be discerned, but more as agenda items to be tested during the sequence of meetings which lead to the relationship being formed. Field observations show the following to be important:

- commitment of top management
- shared vision and goals
- open approach
- willingness to respond
- demonstrated ability
- organisation mapping

The latter means the willingness and ability to establish supplier and customer teams which effectively dovetail with each other, thereby facilitating open and effective dialogue across the interface – a dialogue which would be inhibited if it all had to be conducted through one party on either side. Having said that there is the need to establish two people each 'owning' their side of the relationship: for the supplier this will probably be the Key Account Manager (KAM) and for the customer: the Key Supplier Account Manager (KSAM).

■ Key account management

KAM has traditionally been the preserve of the sales side of business and a Key Account is by definition a customer which is key to the supplier's achievement of their business objectives. Factors such as market share, potential viability in future markets, financial status, rate of growth or decline, etc. are relevant in deciding criticality or otherwise. The profitability of the account is constantly monitored and it is here that there is a major distinction between the Key Account Manager and a Sales Representative whose success will be judged not so much by profit but by numbers of orders taken. The KAM will focus on the total cost of the business and will have considerable decision-making authority, the sales representative will be interested in sales volumes and price, and have little freedom to move from their brief.

Satisfiers

It starts with knowing more about what the seller's 'satisfiers' are. These are the personal goals, targets and needs they have over and above merely winning the order. Indeed 'winning the order' may not always be the priority. For a sales representative it will be, if his or her success is measured by the volume of new business generated. But if the person you meet is labelled a Key Account Manager then their goal will be to achieve a certain level of profitability from the account with the customer. Too many 'special' demands from the customer add to the supplier's cost of servicing the account, and its profitability perhaps falls below the acceptable minimum. So, no sale. Table 15.1 lists some of the things the seller may be looking for. Knowing this gives the buyer a stronger negotiating position when persuading the supplier to offer a lower cost deal.

Table 15.1 Possible seller's objectives

1. Maximise price	12. Earn commission
2. Increase turnover	13. Increase market share
3. Increase volume	14. Acquire new business
4. Increase customer dependency	15. Drive out competition
5. Get sales at end of financial year	16. Meet sales targets
6. Make profit	17. Fill capacity
7. Dump stock	18. Long-term contract
8. Obtain contacts	19. Get 'foot in the door'
9. Product endorsement	20. Interesting work
10. Understand modus operandi	21. Keep a team together
11. Obtain 'inside information'	

The number of customers managed is another major differentiator. Whilst a sales representative may have hundreds of customers a key account manager will typically have 1 to 20. One sales director remarks that 'KAM effectiveness declines rapidly when the number goes beyond single figures'.

'KSAM': key supplier account management

Key Supplier Account Management is now more evident in forward-looking companies and is the direct parallel to KAM. Adapting the KAM role statement reads as follows: 'The KSAM is one who achieves strategic business objectives by managing/ influencing the interface between the key supplier and our company as its customer.' However, the challenge is not so much to define what the KSAM has to do, but to get used to the idea that a very different kind of person is required from the traditional buyer bravely attempting to handle hundreds of suppliers single handedly. Quite apart from dedicating resource to managing perhaps just one supplier, considerable authority is required, not just in the sense of decision-making but also to gather together the different specialists needed during strategic planning and to orchestrate all the personal contacts between the two companies, not least at Board level.

■ References

Smithard, P. M., PMMS Consulting Group Ltd, England.
Russill, R. C. (1992), 'Don't Keep Suppliers at Arm's Length', *Electronic Components*, July, Asian Sources Media Group

Chapter sixteen

Negotiation does not have to mean meeting halfway

The Introduction, point 7 posed the following question:

How would you define negotiation?

Choose the one definition out of the following which most nearly fits your viewpoint:

(a) the act of resolving conflict between two parties
(b) the use of logic to convince the other party
(c) fighting to get your own way
(d) a win/lose process
(e) a process for getting the other party to change its mind
(f) a compromise reached by discussion

No matter where the question is asked in hundreds of negotiation seminars conducted internationally . . . Northern or Southern hemispheres, East or West – the majority of people choose option 'f'. Negotiation is a life skill, not a technique applied only in commercial negotiations, but the popular belief appears to be that compromise is necessary in order to reach agreement. But think of the consequences. Neither party gets exactly what they want since mutual concessions have been made. And the evidence is that compromise agreements hold together whilst things are going well, but that both parties begin to feel dissatisfied when the relationship comes under strain. Compromise *does* have a part to play in negotiation, as does logic, but that is not the whole story. They are just two examples of fundamentally different methods of persuasion which skilled negotiators call on in order to get the other party to change their mind. Answer 'e' above is the correct choice if we are to set our sights high on becoming 'best' negotiators.

■ Not win–win but won-round

But where does the 'win–win' concept fit in? Win–win is widely advised as the ideal goal but, whilst this correctly hints at the feelings which both parties should have about the negotiation's outcome, it wrongly implies 'something for you and something for me' . . . and we're back to compromise and its seductive call to 'meet half way'. Win–win is really about getting the other party to see things your way *and* to feel good about that. It is not about reaching agreement by splitting differences 50–50. Many people think that negotiation automatically involves moving from our ideal position in order to reach agreement. We focus more on how we can persuade people to come away from their position, to come right round to seeing things our way *and* to feel good about being won round. Win–win now becomes 'win–perceived-win' (Steele, Murphy and Russill, 1995) or 'win–won-round'.

Methods of persuasion

Getting people to change their mind can involve up to five different methods of persuasion. The first three are **logic, power and threat**, and **emotion**. All of these are used in high-class companies operating in the most ethical way, the secret lies in how the methods are used. For example, power and threat are often used in an aggressive way and this carries the risk that the other party may call your bluff. As far as emotion is concerned, typically you find people are too inhibited. Emotion does not mean breaking down into tears and having hysterics. Emotion is a 'moving of the feelings' and its power in negotiation is that the use of feelings can create movement. Emotion is all about coming across as a person with feelings. These may be positive: 'I am really pleased with the way this deal is shaping up', or may reflect disappointment: 'I feel that you are exploiting your position with us, Mr Supplier'. Very often you find that people will not say these things. They do not think that expressing feelings is part of the business discussion. And yet the use of emotion – which must reflect genuine feelings if it is to be successful – is one of the biggest contributors to achieving far better results than were otherwise thought to be possible.

Those are the first three methods of persuasion: logic, power and threat, and emotion. One characteristic which they all share is that they can be successful in getting the other party to change position without you having to make concessions as well. But there comes a stage where two-way movement is needed in order to build towards the best negotiation outcome. This involves another persuasion method: **bargaining**. Many people believe that negotiation is *only* about bargaining but, like compromise, the danger here is that we are convincing ourselves that movement on our part is essential – and already we have lost the advantage by not exploring what can first be won by logic and the other 'one-way' persuasion methods.

Bargaining is where there is movement on both sides, but it differs from compromise in that more than one negotiating variable is involved. A compromise between a 10 per cent and a 5 per cent price discount will lie somewhere between these two positions. But a bargain might see the buyer offering a longer-term contract in order to attract a better offer from the supplier. You can now see a bargain in the making: an example of give and take. Finally there is **compromise**, and this should be left until last as the means of bridging the final gap, a gap which has been narrowed significantly by using the other persuasion methods. Once you have moved from your original position using only compromise, the credibility of that position is undermined. There has been no reason to move other than your desire to reach agreement, and the skilled other party will hold ground and let you keep on coming. Left until last, however, especially if the rest of the negotiation has gone very much your way, a small act of compromise may secure the deal simply because it lets the other obtain a small win and enables them to save face with themselves and with the other people in their company who will be looking critically at the outcome. Compromise therefore involves both parties moving towards each other on the same negotiable issue. But get out of the common perception that each must move an equal distance. Going one metre towards the other person, and them coming a kilometre to you, is still compromise.

But, for whoever is moving, there is yet more danger if there is not a very clear target to aim for and to be wary of not reaching.

■ Top targeting . . . and the F-squared factor!

It doesn't matter what targets we are considering – price, lead time, concessions from another party, even a salary raise – the conventional wisdom is 'aim high'. But there the advice stops and there is little suggested to explain how to do it. As a result, people do not win as much as they could and although they do get a deal, there may still be the nagging doubt that they could have got more. So we need to focus thinking on what is wanted, and to increase the chances of getting it. This approach is called 'Top Targeting' (Russill, 1991).

First let us try the following test, which was point 8 in the Introduction:

'You wish to acquire a new personal computer with full multi-media facilities. The make and type has already been decided. Each of three suppliers has offered prices as follows:

Dealer:	A	B	C
Price:	$7,100	$7,300	$7,295
Target:			

Please write down your price target (expressed as a number or a percentage discount) for each dealer, in the spaces provided. Each supplier is offering precisely the same "total" package.'

So what is your answer? Most people's instinctive response is to set a percentage discount target which they hope to achieve, say 10 per cent off. Some go further and calculate this through to a target price: this works out at $6,390, $6,570 and $6,565.5 respectively. What is wrong is now obvious: why target to pay different prices depending on the price asked? Surely the 'same' package is worth the 'same' price irrespective of source – so the first part of Top Targeting is to 'set targets reflecting your needs, rather than what the other party is asking'.

A second point is: do not compromise in your mind when setting targets. Privately you say to yourself 'I'd really like to get "this" but they'd never agree to it so I'll be happy to settle for "that".' This is an assumption but it is treated as a fact, and it will remain an assumed fact until you take the time to test it out on the other party. Who knows, they might have reasons for being able to reach an agreement very much more favourable to you than you thought possible.

One of the 'risks' of Top Targeting is that the more you ask for, the more likely you are to get an astonished reaction (fake or real) from the other party. 'You must be joking!' or 'What ever makes you think that this can be justified?' The point is that there *must* be a credible comeback or it will be clear that you are just 'trying it on', and the attempt to achieve the target falls at the first hurdle. However, do not be too hasty to present detailed logic to support the case or this might reveal a weak point for the other party to attack – and it may also give the impression that you yourself feel that your case is a bit weak because you have to give so much information to support it. A better approach if, for example, you are asking for a very fast delivery, would simply be to say that your company has an urgent order to supply; and then ask the other party what things they can do to achieve your objective. Point 3 then is: 'be prepared with a comeback'. But another danger now emerges. People often limit their targets to what the logic can justify.

Imagine another scenario:

> You have a long-standing relationship with your bank who provide an adequate service for you, but who on several occasions have irritated you by their inefficiency. You recently entered a period of major expenditures and as a result your account became overdrawn some three months ago: call it month 1. This was OK because you have an arrangement with the bank. However, you are now paying interest charges on the overdrawn amount. The expenditures continued and you were even more overdrawn at the beginning of month 2. You are expecting some income in the near future that will offset this overdraft but in order to eliminate the interest charges in the interim you decided, at the beginning of month 2, to sell some stocks and shares and credit the proceeds to your account. These share holdings were sold for you by the bank and you expected the proceeds to enter your account at start of month 3. It is now the end of month 3 and you have received your bank statement, which reveals that *no* sale proceeds have been credited to you. As a result, significant extra interest charges have been made. You immediately call the bank who say that there has been an administrative error but that they will be able to pay in your money any day now. Coming on top of all the other inefficiencies this is the last straw, and you decide that you must meet with the bank manager as soon as possible to complain. Question: what is *your* objective for this meeting: what is *your* target?

The facts would justify you asking the bank manager to repay to you the extra interest charges which have built up during month 3, due to their mistake. If this is your aim, then that is good – remembering that many people would do nothing (not liking to make a fuss) or would ask for 'some' repayment having already told themselves that it would be unreasonable for the bank to repay it all.

But 'Top Targeters' would get more, and did so when this happened in real life. The bank repaid not just the month 3 interest but *also* the interest from months 1 and 2 as a sign of good will, but only after the customer had made a convincing case based on *feelings* (e.g. 'I need you to do something which will make me feel that you really *do* care about me as one of your customers, because up to now all you have given me is a lot of problems'). This is the final and perhaps most powerful aspect of Top Targeting: 'the F-squared factor'. It means basing your targets on *facts* and *feelings*, and not limiting them to what the logic can justify.

■ Phases of negotiating . . . what's going on?

When two or more people meet to negotiate, the first thing they do *not* do is to state their opening positions. They begin by greeting one another, exchange salutations, perhaps enquire of each other's health and the health of each other's businesses. If you know the other party well, you will be interested in their affairs. If you do not know them, you are at least being polite and civil. Many take such formalities for granted, but skilled negotiators realise that this *opening* stage is the first of four distinct phases of the face-to-face part of negotiation. Get it wrong, and the rest of the meeting may be a waste of time.

The **opening** phase is your *only* chance to make a first impression. Wrong impressions given can take hours or several meetings to dispel and the negative feelings in the other party will get in the way of them wanting to agree with you. If you are seen as being impolite or ignoring the usual formalities (which will differ depending on nationalities) you will be seen as 'cold'. It needs warmth to create the rapport which will lead to agreement, but do not come over as 'easy' or the agreement will favour the other party more than you. Aim to be firm but courteous and you will come over as 'warm and tough'.

Still in the opening phase, but after the pleasantries, it is easy to undo the first impression by using non-assertive statements like 'We were rather hoping that you could deliver a little earlier.' Decide what outcomes you want from the negotiation, and link your opening statements to them, e.g. 'We need earlier delivery and this meeting is to explore with you how that can be achieved'. A statement like this also affects the thinking of the other party: it starts to 'condition' their expectations and in their mind they will start backing off from any idea they had about *increasing* delivery time to you. The opening phase therefore is about creating a 'warm–tough' first impression, using opening statements linked to your intended outcome; and conditioning the other party's expectations.

Next is **testing**: test your own assumptions and test how firm the other party's position is *before* revealing yours. Returning to the delivery issue, you will be asked 'How much sooner did you want it?' To answer 'in ten days' will be taken as an initial position by the other party and they will attempt to push you back from it, probably leading to an agreement on more than ten days. Instead, bounce the question back, e.g. 'How much flexibility do you have?' and you may be surprised to hear 'Well, we could deliver in six days for you.' You would never have got that by stating your position first.

As well as testing how flexible the other party could be, now is the time for checking whether any assumptions made during preparation and planning are true or not. Skilled negotiators are skilled interviewers – asking 'open' questions to get the other party talking, 'hypothetical' questions to test the water – and avoid questions which include the answer, such as 'Has your price increased because raw materials have gone up?'. You learn nothing from them! Good questions can be wasted if good listening does not follow: so use silence to digest what you have heard. This also puts pressure on the other party who may then say more than was intended. Also, untangle the code words: someone who says that to agree with you would be 'difficult' is *not* saying that it is 'impossible'. Get information by watching their body language but take care, for although body language can 'speak volumes', it is easy to read it wrongly. After the interviewing, start pushing to test how firm they are in their positions. Skilled negotiators realise that **logic, emotion** and the discrete use of **power and threat** are positive persuaders which may win concessions from the other party without giving any in return.

It is only when testing is exhausted – and the other party may show this, as frustration creeps into their body language – that you should edge into the **moving** phase. Many wrongly believe that this is where negotiation starts and finishes. To believe this is to have a limited perception of the process and encourages people to believe that we can only get agreement by making concessions. This ignores the excellent gains which can be made in the testing phase. However, these may not be enough and the moving phase is the time for **bargaining** (exchanging different concessions) and finally **compromise** (agreeing on a final position between two different points on the same negotiable issue).

Whether things have gone well or not the final phase of the meeting is **agreeing**. If final agreement has not been reached then at least agree on what progress has been made and what the next steps should be. This establishes the common ground from which to start the next meeting. If a deal has been reached then, before 'shaking' on it, skilled negotiators retain control by carefully summarising their understanding of what has been agreed, and seeking agreement to the summary. Or they may still exert control by asking the other party to summarise. Their control also stops them from the conditioned reflex to shake hands too soon or to fall for the 'just one more thing' tactic!

■ Four characteristics of successful negotiators

Successful negotiation comes down to four things. One is **confidence and belief** in what you are trying to achieve. A clear idea of your target or point of view is essential if you want to persuade the other party to share it. Lacking confidence and belief will do two things to damage your case. Any lack of confidence will betray itself in your body language and will also be evident in unassertive verbal behaviour. Also, the lack of belief will take away from the feelings with which you convey your case. If you really believe something, you will communicate with a passion which will have an effect on your listener. Not really believing makes the speech as mechanistic as if reading from someone else's script. Another key characteristic is that a skilled negotiator is a **skilled person-watcher**. An enormous amount of information can be gained by observing the behaviour of the other party: the body language and the way they respond to situations. Skilled negotiators both see and can analyse this. You have got to be in two places at once. Part of you has to be at the negotiating table presenting the case, the other part hovers like a video camera taking a cool, uninvolved look at what is going on.

A third point: successful negotiators are **likeable**. Much effort has to go in to create the rapport, to make the person feel that they want to help you. That is a skill: how to be liked by the other person without crawling up to them or being subservient. We look for the 'warm–tough' behaviour set. Warm–easy offers no challenge and cold–tough creates hostile reactions. You do not get best and long-lasting deals by terrorising them out of the other party.

The fourth characteristic of successful negotiators is that they can **manage themselves and the situation** in the heat of debate. They never lose sight of their ultimate (and, incidentally, extremely ambitious) objective, but may show considerable flexibility in the route they have to take to reach it. Reaching your objective via their route is another way of looking at win–won-round.

Negotiation is not just something for the office but is a life skill in the sense that you are constantly surrounded by negotiable opportunities, and most days need to get someone thinking your way. It is a life skill in that the skills have been with you for life. Young children show considerable negotiating skill but we allow our adult inhibitions, and often the culture of the office, to reduce effectiveness to a mere fraction of what it was and can again be. So, for many people, negotiating training is often a voyage of rediscovery.

■ References

Steele, Paul, John Murphy and Richard Russill (1995), *It's a Deal*, McGraw-Hill.

Russill, R. C. (1991), 'Set targets to get the best deal possible', *Electronic Components*, September, Asian Sources Media Group, Hong Kong.

Chapter seventeen

How to measure procurement impact

The problem with the whole topic of 'measuring procurement effectiveness' is that the issue is muddled. Many companies are mired in self-doubt and look to measures of value-added and cost saving to decide whether in-house procurement is worth doing at all, or whether the whole activity should be outsourced to a contractor. In contrast the best companies accept that procurement is essential to the success of the business, with the attention then going on how to make as good as possible a job of it, measuring performance improvement along the way.

Measurement should be straightforward, with the following goals:

- to track the efficiency and effectiveness of the procurement effort, both as an organisational entity and as a contributor to corporate teamwork
- to provide a basis for setting targets and as the vehicle for feedback by which individual staff may be held accountable for achieving results to which they have previously committed themselves
- to ensure that procurement effort is focussed on those activities which provide best returns for the effort and expertise invested
- to identify areas requiring improvements or remedial action, or which provide opportunity to get new wins

Reality tends to be different. The muddle arises because, in a world of reengineered processes, tight control and 'management by numbers', people look for 'numbers' (ideally just one) to answer several measurement questions simultaneously:

- how good is our order-placing activity compared with others?
- are we meeting our targets?
- are we getting the best prices?
- is procurement justifying its existence in the first place?

The last two concerns have been dealt with elsewhere in this book (chapters 12 and 3 respectively). But, whilst all these questions are valid, the problem is that some are matters of core belief, not lending themselves to easy proof by mathematical analysis.

For example, we can run some numbers to calculate when, in a growing company, it becomes worthwhile to create a position of 'full time buyer'. Let us assume that the presence of dedicated resource, as opposed to several people doing it part time, less effectively and less 'knowingly', will achieve an overall 10 per cent reduction in supply-side costs. It depends on local wage rates, but to justify the total compensation package for a suitably qualified person would require a supply-side spend in excess of half a million pounds for the investment in the person to be fully returned by the straight savings made. This ignores the other benefits arising due to time being released for the other people to do other things. Many would now get into debating the figures: 10 per cent? – more or less? How much to pay for the right person? And this is exactly the pitfall of the numbers. They, and the whole calculations-based approach, suggest that it is optional whether or not procurement is taken seriously. If the return is not high enough then the dedication of expertise (full- or part-time) is not worth it. Or, as it is more often put in fat companies wanting to get lean: 'It is costing too much, let's contract it out and cut costs that way.' Immersion in the mathematics clouds the real issue, which is that 'being in business' automatically means being into 'supply-side management'. The real questions then revolve around how best to do it as part of the total company effort to achieve corporate goals. To seek to justify procurement's existence as an isolated function is like trying to prove whether or not you need fuel to make fire.

Besides, corporate excellence is not proved simply by demonstrating cost effectiveness: other parameters such as return on capital, cash flow, stock price, external reputation for business integrity and innovation, shareholder loyalty, etc. all come into the equation. Focus on these as the real numbers to go for and ensure that each contributor to that effort, including procurement, has clear plans and targets clearly linked to these corporate needs. This way the whole is greater than the sum of the parts, and procurement is clearly seen as inherently relevant to the business rather than as an expensive clerical burden.

Many texts and papers are published in the attempt to prove things mathematically. One article, published in a journal which should have known better, even sought to explain procurement's importance in terms of the amount of incoming sales revenue it expended. The higher the better! And an observed trend in one industry sector where purchasing expenditures were falling as a percentage of sales income was despairingly seen as evidence that purchasing was losing its grip!

But amidst all the data and the debate, two key questions are usually ignored, answers to which must be the starting point for any sensible way through the maze. They are:

1. Who's interested?
2. What are you trying to prove?

The easy bit is to suggest specific measures which can be tracked. Appendix 17.1 provides a menu. But the greater challenge is to address the above questions and then to make the right menu selection. This is because there is no one 'right' answer about what to measure: the answers will differ for different managers and different companies, depending on where they are at the time in question and what they are trying to achieve. To heap measures on to the 'monthly reporting' plate in the hope that something will satisfy will only cause data indigestion, and will certainly not give senior-management recipients clear signals about the relevance of procurement activity. So measurement itself is a moving target, and what is right to measure will change and become more strategic as the stature of procurement impact evolves in terms of the results achieved and the attitudes and support of others at all levels in the company whose collaboration is an intrinsic part of the success.

It is also necessary to distinguish between efficiency and effectiveness. High efficiency equates with minimised effort on low-value tactical activity, quick and accurate responses to others' legitimate needs, lean manning, low operating costs and effective support systems. High effectiveness reflects the impact made by the buyer in shaping and enhancing the cross-functional procurement process, the impact of that process on corporate performance and the degree to which the external supply market is influenced and changed to the buying company's advantage. Efficiency needs to be measured and improved first as the precursor of full effectiveness.

■ Who's interested?

To be worth the measurement effort, performance must be tracked and reported in terms which interest the recipient and which are perceived by them to be relevant. Several points spring from this.

1. **Different recipients need different measures** Any manager should certainly be tracking internal costs and efficiency as part of their normal line-management responsibility to control and to improve to meet new targets. But too much emphasis on this from the boss or the boss's boss signifies an unhealthy suspicion that the purchasing activity is a burden on the business. Better for them to be advised on the progress being made to develop and implement new acquisition strategies or other developments aimed at enhancing effectiveness, and for the CEO to hear about similar issues but on a larger scale (e.g. the degree to which individual businesses within a worldwide group of companies are participating in global strategies; or the progress being made against specific financial targets or against specific actions whose completion is essential to the achievement of some other corporate goal).

2. **The measures you report have a direct impact on people's perceptions of what procurement there is to do** The corollary is that the measures asked for by senior management are good indicators of the value (if any) they place on the activity. Table 17.1 illustrates four different perceptions of procurement's role, the resulting measurement focus and examples of what might be measured. Obviously we want to get to the 'top' but this may mean starting at the bottom.

Many regard procurement as a low status, clerical, order-placement activity. In this 'overhead-cost' oriented environment, procurement's contribution will neither be understood nor measured in positive terms. The cost of running the function will be all too evident and measurement will focus on 'inputs', i.e. the resources which have to be provided to sustain the activity as tracked by headcount and operating costs.

Table 17.1 Different viewpoints

Current view	Measurement focus	Example of measurement
Essential for business success	Competitive advantage	Financial targets Strategy coverage
Contributor', but needing to prove	Profit impact	'Savings'
Service	Outputs	Response time Stock availability
An 'overhead'	Inputs	Budgets/headcount

Suppose though that the order-placers are now regarded as providing a useful service. Measurement now focusses on the 'outputs', i.e. the results of buyers' efforts and reflects the quality of service provided, response times, stock availability, etc. Going further, many organisations find themselves in this situation but wish to improve in order to make profit or value-for-money contributions. Those to whom the order-placers report are partially convinced of the incentives to change but 'need proof'. This leads to measurement of cost savings and the like. For these to be credible, cost avoidance (e.g. a wholly or partially resisted price increase) must not be confused with the far more attractive aim of actual cost reduction where less is paid now than before.

Finally we arrive at the desirable situation where procurement's role is both understood and valued by senior management. There is now as much regard for contribution to profit/value-for-money as there is for the role that the procurement process plays in optimising company exposure to the supply market. Measurement focusses on the strategic contribution made: less exposure to market distortions, input to make or buy decisions, development of supply market choices and responses which are consistent with what the business needs overall to succeed. Financial impact is not now measured as an isolated outcome of procurement activity (e.g. as savings) but as a consequence of a process in which different functions have implemented specific actions which together add up to a target-achieving performance, with these financial forecasts built into the projections of profitability for the current fiscal year.

3. **Stretch, but stay in touch with, people's perceptions** It is important that the measures reported are 'within reach' of the recipient's perceptions. If not, they will be seen as irrelevant. For example, to report in terms of the 'quality of procurement process' to a recipient who sees order-placing as an undesirable but inevitable drain on resources will invite charges of being out of touch and going soft. Even 'savings' may be dismissed as 'funny money', especially if the company is in a loss-making phase. If headcount and internal budget performance is what is asked for, then give it – but at the same time 'piggy back' on it an additional piece of reportage which is designed to expand the recipient's perception, for example an innovation achieved by collaborating with a supplier. That way the buyer has a chance of weaning the

recipient on to an aspect of performance which is more interesting and strategic. Relevance is in the eye of the recipient, so play their tune to start with but then introduce some variations to deepen their appreciation.

■ What are we trying to prove?

The answer is not that procurement should be recognised as an enabler for business. Yes, this is the fact but, no, mere numbers will never prove it. To do this needs a story – something along the lines of that told in chapter 3. What is to be proved by the measurement process is whether or not things are under control, that sufficient progress is being made towards targets, that change and continual improvement is happening fast enough, and that supply markets are now beginning to respond in the way we need them to. Again it is up to each manager to choose not only the measures which are right for their situation but, before that, the definition of what is important in the first place. Fortunately, Supply Positioning can be deployed as illustrated below.

Many of these measures are 'internally relevant' to the procurement team but still have an external focus. This means that the measures are primarily there to help with the direction and control of procurement activity whilst maintaining an emphasis on supply market and supplier management issues (as distinct from being overly inward looking). They are also focussed on specific procurement tasks, but what can one start measuring as early indicators of the quality of process, recognising its cross-business multi-specialist nature?

The following are suggested as first steps:

1. **Measures to gauge efficiency and control**:
   total expenditures for the company showing the split between those made by procurement and by non-procurement personnel. Some of these will have been properly delegated to users but the figures must also highlight the (often considerable) activities taking place outside of any influence of the procurement process.
   requisitions, commitments and expenditures to date, reported per buyer. This includes expenditures made by non-buyers using delegated authorities or by other means such as procurement cards or call-offs from supply contracts
   expenditures grouped by major suppliers and major spend areas
   time taken to place key orders
   percentage of total contracts made having a traceable formal approval or requisition
   percentage of total contracts made on the basis of buyer's terms and conditions
   invoice queries referred to originating buyers, as an absolute number and as a percentage of invoices received
   price increases requested and the negotiated outcome (including approval controls)
   procurement operating cost (sometimes referred to as 'the cost of buying') as an absolute number and as percentage of total supply-side expenditure

Strategic security	Strategic critical
Goal: Ensure supplies	*Goal:* Close supply management
Examples of Measures: Cycle times Degree of EDI usage Forecasting accuracy Delivery accuracy Inventory management Supplier responsiveness Quality and rejects Contingency plans	*Examples of measures:* Profit contribution Supplier performance Costs versus financial targets No of supplier visits Innovations No. of source options No. of strategic plans
Tactical acquisition	**Tactical profit**
Goal: Minimum attention	*Goal:* More profit/VFM
Examples of measures: No. of orders versus no. of items No. of sources Percentage items covered by delegated Purchasing or call-offs Cost of purchasing	*Examples of measures:* Degree of standardisation Direct cost savings Re-sourcing rate Sourcing research Stock turn

2. **Measures to gauge procurement effectiveness**

time spent per buyer moving forward on critical/strategic items as opposed to tactical items, claims or problem resolution

percentage of buyer time spent on 'strategic upstream' activity

percentage of tactical acquisition items not requiring direct hands-on buyer involvement

emergency or 'rush' items (has implications re user attitudes and effectiveness)

savings (conforming to predetermined definitions and reported for each buyer) made against price targets built into financial forecast

percentage of all (apart from tactical acquisition items) needs which have been subjected to an organised, process-facilitated, multi-specialist strategic planning activity

percentage of all (apart from tactical acquisition items) needs where buyers have automatically been involved in user budget-planning sessions, augmented by controlled supplier contacts, for next fiscal year's key supply-side needs

if there is no procurement 'department' as such, the degree to which commerciality is ingrained in the minds and behaviours of all who have supply-side contact and interaction

As for senior management, rather than looking for 'savings' one would expect their interest in cost issues to be met in their review of overall company financial performance, albeit clearly showing what specific targets are for delivery via the procurement process. They would then be acutely aware of, and positively interested in, the strategic-critical issues, notably the risk-management aspects and the progress being made implementing strategies designed to change supply market behaviour to that needed by the corporate strategy and as defined by the Supply-Planning process.

The measurement hierarchy

Having taken a look at an objectively put-together measurement structure, what do we actually find companies doing in practice? Table 17.2 illustrates.

Again starting from the bottom of the list, many are involved with **internal benchmarking**. This means comparing different sites within the company, using various indices for comparison purposes. These include items like manpower (total, and per pound or dollar spent; order-placement operating costs; manpower per 1,000 transactions; invoice costs; etc.). The aim is to identify best performance levels and then encourage each site to achieve them. One company adopted golfing terminology and introduced the idea of 'pars'. No one wanted to be 'below par' and this stimulated some improvement effort. But such internal comparisons can be incestuous, and how do we set 'pars' in the first place which reflect best practice anywhere, not just inside our company?

Recognition of this explains the recent trend towards **external benchmarking**, which focusses on similar data but this time shared between several companies who may or may not be from the same industry sector. Internal and external benchmarking certainly involves a lot of work but is not guaranteed to be useful. Often the cry is 'OK, so we've got the data, but what is it telling us?' Perhaps this is the real benefit: it stimulates the asking of questions, although most of them will be functionally inward-looking and be fixated on 'How can we do things with fewer resources?' It can also create negative competition between sites, with data being massaged or selectively

Table 17.2 A measurement hierarchy

. . . if you do believe, then no proof is necessary	
Best-Practice Profiling	] Process
Quality of internal process	]
Contribution – to corporate strategy	) Outputs
– to specific tasks	)
Performance indices (e.g. 'savings')	) Outputs
Price 'index' comparisons	)
Service indicators	)
External benchmarking (inputs)	} Inputs
Internal benchmarking (inputs)	}
*'If you **do not** believe, then no proof is possible . . .'*	

reported in order to look good. In any case, a lot of data processing is needed to ensure that apples are being compared with apples. The great danger with benchmarking is that the process can become an end in itself and, even if there is enough energy left over to take actions, there are few clues as to how to improve things. This is because the focus is on inputs, i.e. the resources being deployed to do the work. Comparisons are only valid if the work is identical. However, the issues being measured (e.g. budgets, headcount) are very much the concern of the procurement manager, and internal benchmarking provides market intelligence which assists in the running and improving of the activity for which they are responsible. This is a valid reason for internal benchmarking, but things start to go wrong when it is used as a comparative tool to 'score' absolute effectiveness.

What can be more meaningful is to compare outputs, i.e. the results produced by the team effort. **Service indicators** such as order-processing times, stock availability, quality of the product or service supplied, etc., come into this category. Quite apart from being highly relevant to the internal users, service indicators can also be regarded as rudimentary measures of the 'process capability' of the buyer team, although better process measures (see below) address the overall procurement process in a cross-functional sense. A very customer-oriented buyer team may initiate customer-service measures. (Figure 17.1 illustrates the results of a customer-service survey conducted across the 28-site European operations of a multi-national company.)

Such measures can be useful during the early stages of a change programme designed to promote a different image for purchasing and to achieve better collaboration between buyers and users. It is interesting that the customers of figure 17.1 give high scores for the service-efficiency aspects, whereas the more strategic attributes (e.g. creativity and market knowledge) are lower rated. Perhaps the buyers are not 'up' to that or maybe the customers do not expect it. If the latter is the case, we are left to wonder what that company is doing to change perceptions. The problem of over-use of customer surveys is that they perpetuate the idea that the 'customer is king' and that order-placers are there merely to satisfy their every whim. This runs counter to the view that procurement is a cross-functional process essential for the success of the business as distinct from being a service fighting for the loyalty of customers who might otherwise satisfy their supply market needs in other ways.

Returning to table 17.2, the focus on the commercial aspects of the buyer's job is at least recognised by the use of **price 'index' comparisons**. Agencies are available to which subscribers regularly submit data about the prices they have paid for certain items they buy (e.g. utilities, fuel, chemicals). The agency collates the data and gives out to the subscriber a spreadsheet showing where their prices sit alongside those paid by other (unidentified) subscribers. Criticisms of such price comparisons concern the suspicion that the data may be flawed because subscriber companies do not always declare the best prices they paid, plus the fact that over-reliance on such data to 'prove' that procurement is doing a good job merely perpetuates the image that the main aim is to achieve the lowest price. Like inputs-benchmarking, price comparisons are mainly useful when viewed as providing market intelligence about trends and general price levels rather than as a tool for measuring effectiveness.

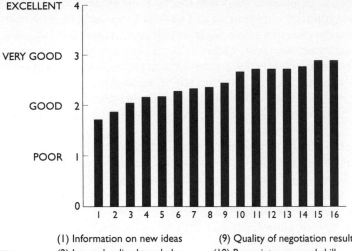

(1) Information on new ideas   (9) Quality of negotiation results
(2) Internal policy knowledge   (10) Buyer interpersonal skill
(3) Buyer's market knowledge   (11) Buyer availability
(4) Supplier delivery dates   (12) Quality of service, reliability
(5) Supplier quality   (13) Follow-up, expediting
(6) Quality of purchase request   (14) Buyer profit-sensitivity
(7) Image of purchasing   (15) Promptness of processing
(8) Quality of goods/services   (16) Accuracy of purchase order

Figure 17.1 Internal customer service survey

A step up the ladder is to broaden the issue and focus on total costs and savings. These are examples of what can be labelled as '**performance indices (savings)**', since they are more holistic measures reflecting what has been achieved through broader thinking by buyers and their internal company colleagues. Savings, providing they are credible and seen as the result of internal teamwork, are useful in capturing the attention of those who might previously have seen purchasing merely as about order-placement. A quantifiable value adding contribution is now evident. Measuring savings in one part of the company can provide helpful case histories for others to follow. They can also demonstrate the characteristics and benefits of strategic procurement and how this differs from reactive buying.

In discussing table 17.2, the theme that now begins to emerge is that any particular measure has its place at a certain time and prepares the way for moving to a different measure when appropriate. So it is with savings. A company that views its procurement operation as a valuable contributor to profit is a long way forward from seeing it as the regulator of order-placement. But still there is room to develop perceptions beyond 'just' profit contribution and there will come a time when, having served its purpose, 'savings' reporting takes a lower profile to be replaced not so much by routine measures but by reports on how the procurement process is making an impact in a broader sense.

Contribution . . . to specific tasks (e.g. shorter new-product development, dramatic reduction in equipment outage time) and to delivering the corporate strategy overall (e.g. establishment of new sources in geographic areas where it is intended to create a presence in new markets; contribution to liquidity by negotiating favourable credit terms with major suppliers) continue to develop perceptions and show that strategic procurement activity can enhance competitive advantage.

So far our concern has been with inputs and outputs. Highest level measures go further still, being concerned with the process within the company which converts inputs into outputs: i.e. resources into results.

Measuring the **quality of internal process** is the priority of companies who firmly believe that it requires excellent processes of interaction between people and functions in order to achieve best task results. Indeed, the very idea of functionality will be receding in favour of giving people multi-dimensional roles. The different steps in the procurement process are connected together and can be regarded as a pipeline of activity with sample points between each step. At each sample point, the 'ideal' process can be defined, e.g. how would we recognise an excellent process leading to a high-quality statement of need (requisition). Actual behaviours monitored or 'sampled' will then be compared against these standards in order to detect the shortfalls. This leads to actions which close the gap. At a critical stage in its programme of change to build an excellent procurement process one company made tremendous impact by concentrating its main measurement effort, as reported to senior management, on just two issues: performance against the 'standard procurement process' and costs savings achieved and publicised as a 'credible teamwork success'.

Now we are back to a question asked at the outset: 'What does it look like outside?' But this time the focus is not on numbers of people and comparative costs but at a much deeper level. **Best-Practice Profiling** gets beneath the surface of inputs and outputs and tests a company organisation against defined criteria which profile the internal environment and which, if met, mean that 'best practice' becomes reality. Issues tested include the policy and procedural framework, influence of the senior procurement executive, overall organisation of the procurement team effort, systems and strategic planning tools which make up the organisation's infrastructure and competence of staff and their selection processes. The criteria are independently set and compiled from a number of sources (e.g. generally accepted principles of effective management in a knowledge-based empowering age; observed practices of successful companies) and so a company's procurement process and its enabling environment can be assessed on a 'stand-alone' basis or, if desired, compared with others. The critical point is that all companies are being assessed against external standards, thus avoiding the artificiality of declaring as the epitome of best practice the company which just happens to be 'best' of the group under test.

■ The bottom line . . . and the last word

Measurement is a dynamic concept. Precise measures depend on where a company is along the road towards creating a high-performing procurement process and, through careful selection, the measures chosen at one stage can assist progression to the next, using the 'piggy back' principle mentioned earlier. Choosing the measures depends on the current answers to the two key questions: 'Who's interested?' and 'What are we trying to prove?'

But how do we respond to those who say 'there's no answer to the question of how to quantify and measure procurement effectiveness'? If there was a numerical index then this would be the lazy person's way of explaining and justifying procurement's worth. Reality presents a different challenge because there is no one number that can replace the advocacy needed to tell a compelling story which convinces people that the procurement process is an intrinsic part of being in business, and not some optional activity that is tolerated only for as long as it is able to pay its way with cost savings.

Moses did not get people to cross the Red Sea because he had calculated and proved for them that real estate values were better on the other side. He talked instead of 'a Promised Land'. And that brings us to the words which top and tail table 17.2. They were used to conclude a radio interview with a scientist who had calculated that, given a certain set of wind and tide conditions, it was logical that the waters of the Red Sea could have parted. But the real message was in the punch line: 'If you don't believe it happened then no proof will convince you, but if you do believe then no proof is necessary.' Which really says it all about the procurement measurement topic. The effort then can be devoted exclusively to doing the job as well as possible as measured by process effectiveness and by the company's success in meeting its financial goals.

■ Appendix   Measurement 'à la carte'

A menu of options based on table 17.2: The Measurement Hierarchy

Core data

Total annual expenditures: company as a whole
                            committed directly by buyers
                            committed indirectly under delegated arrangements
Total annual capital expenditure
Actual expenditures v. total commitments in any time period
Number of contracts made in time period
Order v. value distribution
Number of 'low-value' orders (e.g. less than £3,000)
Percentage of total contracts on own terms and conditions
Number of suppliers: total 'on the books'
                      total 'active'
Suppliers with whom total annual expenditure exceeds £X00,000
Total expenditures in domestic market (if 'local content' is an issue) or other politically sensitive areas

Inputs

Number of buyers
Total number of procurement staff
Operating budget
Equivalent number of 'buyers' elsewhere in company who are internal users with authority to commit
Cost per order raised and invoice paid

Service-indicators

Actual needs v. user forecasts of requirements
Total requisitions handled
Percentage of total requisitions which are defective (e.g. not properly authorised) on receipt
Number of requisitions processed within a given time
Cycle time: duration between requisition, commitment, delivery, payment for regular needs
Number of rebids required (due to errors, changes, etc.)
Percentage of total orders covered by call-off agreements
Percentage of total orders covered by delegated actions (direct authority; procurement cards, etc.)
Number of requirements changed after contract placement
Delivery quality, timeliness, accuracy v. supplier's commitment (contractual and 'promised')
Defects and rejects
Stock-outs
Internal customer satisfaction
Waiting time for salespeople visits
Percentage of total contracts paid as per agreed payment terms

Price indicators

Number of price changes (up or down) from previous prices paid
Frequency of price changes for specific items
Number of price increases challenged and accepted/reduced/deferred/eliminated
Number of price decreases initiated by supplier
Price trends: own products/services v. input prices
                        prices paid to suppliers v. their input prices
Prices achieved v. specific price targets
Prices paid v. published market prices, or v. price-comparison surveys
Variances from standard costs
Year-on-year real-cost reduction
Percentage of total high-spend items which have been price-analysed and 'cost-modelled'

Performance indices: supplier performance

Total hours expediting
Rework costs
Performance v. key expectations
Number of relevant suppliers engaged in continual improvement programs

Performance indices: savings

Percentage of total orders (other than low value) placed in competitive environment
Cost savings realised by:

- changing source(s)
- changing method or timing of approaching the market
- substituting alternatives
- changing specification
- standardisation, leading to volume leverage
- optimised packaging/delivery/inventory costs
- additional value being provided for same price
- using pre-used or surplus items
- concessions (leading to current cost reduction) won by direct negotiation
- initiating price decrease strategies
- improving payment terms
- initiation of end-of-contract rebates
- profitable disposal of written off assets

Contribution: to specific results

Prices paid versus financial plan

Contribution: to corporate strategy and risk management

Percentage of total strategic critical items for which supply positioning, supplier preference and vulnerability analyses have been conducted
Number of strategic plans in place, including contingency measures
Number of monopoly or cartel situations detected and circumvented
Number of alternative sources established and used
Number of alternative services or products identified and acceptable to internal users
Number of successful instances of reverse marketing and procurement marketing
Percentage of strategic-critical items relocated to tactical-profit

Best practice profiling

Contribution and influence
Relationships

Procurement and audit framework
Organisation
Systems
Staff and training

Index

Acquisition planning, 28, 53
Affirmative Vendor Improvement
    Programs (AVIP), 111, 151

Barriers blocking change, 91
Best deals, how to recognise, 124
Best practice, current
    mission for procurement process, 62
    policies and principles, 62
    v. better practice, 10
Bid evaluation, 126
Boundaryless companies, new frontiers in,
    85
BPR, *see* Business Process Re-Engineering
Business
    beginnings of, 8
    getting smaller, problems of, 12
    growth, problems of, 10, 11
    model of, 31
    revival of, 6
    survival, 19
    trends, 17
Business Process Re-Engineering, 88, 89
    downside of, 85
Buyers
    role in future, 23, 70

Cartels, 147
    testing for, 148
    overcoming, 148
Centralised procurement, 71
Centre-Led Action Network, *see* CLAN
'Centrepreneur', 14
Change
    barriers to, 91
    checklist for procurement renaissance,
        94
    critical mass for, 92

incomplete, problems of, 94
    route map for revolution, 76
    tragedy of, 89
Changes and claims, 57
CLAN organisation, 27, 73
    as alternative to centralised/
        decentralised, 73
    benefits of, 77
    network team role, 74
    prerequisites for success, 75
    team leader role, 75
Coca-Cola CEO, 60
Commercial exposure, 25
Common assumptions about procurement,
    32
Competition
    for growth, 17
    for cost reduction, 18
    for hearts and minds, 18
Conditioning, 138
Contract award, 56, 126
Contractual exposure, 25
Contribution to
    corporate strategy, 38
    profit, 34
    task results, 36
Core beliefs about procurement, 20
    access to suppliers, 21
    cross-business teamwork, 22
    image and approach, 26
    tools, techniques, systems and controls,
        27
    value of procurement process, 28
Corporate governance, 27
corporate strategy, 38
Cost curves
    bad, 25
    best, 50

Cost curves (*continued*)
   good, 24
Cost cutting, danger of, 59
Cost reduction strategies
   control, focus and co-ordination, 47
   collaboration with suppliers, 49
   understanding and outmanoeuvring
      supply markets, 48
Cost-time profiles, 156
Cost, wasted, 52, 149
Cover prices, 147
Cross-functional teamwork, 23
   evolution of, 84
   in strategic planning, 103
Culture change, 13
Customers, 30
Customer, internal service survey, 175

Decentralised procurement, 72
Downstream activity
   problems, 69
   time spent on, 69

Empowerment, 86, 88
Exposure
   commercial, 25
   contractual, 25
   legal, 25

'F-squared' factor, 162
FASTRACK checklist for strategic
     planning, 104
Finance function, 44

Hard money, 126
High-performing organisations,
     characteristics, 152

Image, 119, 137
Interest cycling, 114
Internal users, 44

Key Account Manager, 157
Key Supplier Account Manager, 157

Lead buyer, 74
Legal exposure, 25
Leverage, tactical, 90
Local buying, 72

Make versus Buy, 114
Managing suppliers, ten questions, 118
Market intelligence sources, 119

Measurement 'à la carte', 177
Measurement goals, 167
   indicators related to perceptions, 170
   what are we trying to prove?, 171
   who's interested, 169
Measurement hierarchy, 173
Measurement options
   benchmarking (external), 173
   benchmarking (internal), 173
   best practice profiling, 176
   contribution, 176
   price comparisons, 174
   quality of process, 176
   savings, 175, 177
   service indicators, 174
Monopolies
   why they arise, 146
   how to deal with them, 147

Needs specification, 41, 52
Negotiating variables, 134
Negotiation
   definition of, 160
   methods of persuasion, 161
   top-targeting, 162
   win-win vs won-round, 160
Negotiation phases
   agreeing, 165
   moving, 165
   opening, 164
   testing, 164
Negotiators, successful characteristics, 165
'NICE' strategy formula, 102

Order-value distribution, 123
Organisation
   centralised, 71
   CLAN networks, 73
   decentralised, 72
   high performing characteristics, 152
   options, 70
   process oriented, 82
   task oriented, 78
Organisational effectiveness, 66
   defined, 79
Organising
   process leadership, 86
   procurement tasks, 70
   time and priorities, 67

Policies
   best practice list, 63
   what can go wrong?, 67

Positive costs, 29
Pre-eminent organisational effectiveness, 79
Price
  comparisons, 174
  logic, danger of, 135
  future, management of, 143
  not fixed, 34
  plateau, 140
  policies, 135
  proposals, improvement of, 140
  variation formulae, 143
'Priceberg', 47
Process leadership, orchestrating it, 82, 86
Procurement
  and revival of business, 10
  as instrument of change, 80
  best-practice mission, 62
  cards, 68
  core beliefs about, 20
  problems if not organised, 5
  as regulator and controller, 34
  role statement, 60
  shared process, 43
  specialism or influencer?, 16
  task sequence, 41
Procurement Marketing, 22, 114
Procurement process
  characteristics of high quality, 39
  how wasted costs get in, 52
  leadership of, 82, 86
  main stages, 44
  as microcosm of business, 66
  strategic purpose of, 60
Procurement Renaissance, 15
  checklist for change, 94
  route map for revolution, 76
  tangibility of change, 86
  what's required?, 91
Profit contribution, 35
Profit & Loss statements, new look, 30
Purchase tactics, 123

Relationships, 151
Renaissance, see Procurement Renaissance
Reverse marketing, 115

Sellers' satisfiers, 158
Selling the vision, 33
Soft money, 126
Specifying needs, 41

Strategic plan
  'FASTRACK' approach, 104
  'NICE' formula, 102
  position paper, 100
  positioning statements, 101
  template, 100
Strategic Procurement, 39, 90
  compared with Tactical Leverage, 90
  definition of, 40
  evidence of, 40
Supplier
  appraisal, 120, 151, 156
  collaboration, 156
  contacts, 121
  control of, 127
  debriefing, 113
  demotivating them, 154
  importance of, 122
  motivating higher performance, 155
  performance, 128, 154
  relationships, 151, 157
Supplier preference overview, 108
Supply interface, ten key questions, 118
Supply market trends, 17
Supply Positioning, 106
Survival, 19

Tactical Leverage, 90
Target setting, 162
Task
  organisations, 78
  tradition, 78
Ten questions, 118
Ten(d) to Zero, 151
Time
  expenditure pattern, 69
  spent on small orders, 68
Total cost, 35, 133
  elements, 133
  of bad behaviour, 46
  of ownership, 46
Total Quality, 88

Upstream management, 81, 103
  steps defined, 81

Vision of strategic procurement, 64
  stairway to, 33
Vulnerability analysis, 109

Winners and losers, 17